# Reading, Writing and Maths For Self Employment

## Basic Business Planning

*Written and Compiled by*
*Glennys Davis and Patrick Scriven*
*on behalf of Breathing Space Ltd as part of*
*Euro Enterprise Evolutions*



EUROPEAN UNION
European Social Fund

Euro Enterprise Evolutions
Business creation for all

Equal

Breathing Space Ltd

*This product has been part funded by the ESF under the Equal Community Initiative Programme. The contents do not necessarily reflect the opinion or position of the European Commission or the Department for Work and Pensions*

Breathing Space Ltd

# Reading, Writing and Maths for Self Employment

**Published by**

Breathing Space Ltd
The Central Hall
Ablewell Street
Walsall WS1 2EQ

Tel 01922 647696
Fax 01922 628593
Email **enquiries@breathingspaceltd.co.uk**



Breathing Space Ltd

# Reading, Writing and Maths for Self Employment

## Basic Business Planning

## You have an idea for a Business?

**We hope that this book will help with your business planning.**

*For more worksheets look out for*

**Reading, Writing and Maths for Self Employment**

## Workbook

Whilst every effort has been made to ensure that the content of the Toolkit is correct Breathing Space and Euro Enterprise Evolutions are not responsible for any mistakes.

**A Note about Copyright**



If you have purchased this book you may make copies of any pages marked with this icon Copy

# You have an idea for a Business?

**Great!**
**I'm Business Birdie.**
**I'm here to help you find out how to do a simple business plan.**

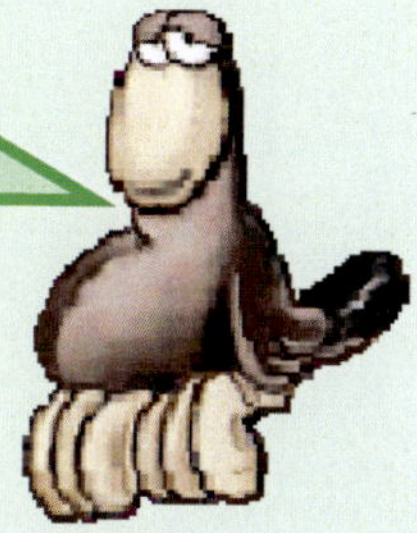

**You need to do a Business Plan if you want to borrow money (loan) or get a grant to set up a business**

## Contents

**The Business Plan for Claire's Cakes will show you how a plan can look.**

Page 8 GO

# Business Plan for Claire's Cakes

## CV

| | |
|---|---|
| Name | Claire Baker |
| Address | 113 Treacle Terrace<br>Battenberg<br>Swiss Cottage |
| Post Code | SW9 99OZ |
| Telephone | 01284846209 |
| Mobile | 07768263018 |
| Date of Birth | 29/06/1976 |
| Driving Licence | Clean (no points) licence |

**Personal Profile**

I have enjoyed baking my own cakes and pastries since childhood. I have run a cake stall at the local market and school and church fetes. I'm a very good time keeper and can talk with people at all levels. I also find it easy to make people feel welcome.

**Skills/Training**

**September 1993 - July 1995**
GB College of Further Education, Learn Lane, Greater Barryville, L3 4RN.
NVQ Levels 2 and 3 in Food Preparation Passed

**July 2006**
GB College
Basic Health and Safety, Food Hygiene Courses taken and passed.

# Business Plan for Claire's Cakes

## CV

### Work History

**April 1998 - January 2006** Shop Manager

Creamy Cakes, High Street, Great Barry, B08 6BB. Duties included every day running of High Street cake shop.

**September 1992 - April 1998** Counter Staff (Part Time)

Creamy Cakes, High Street, Great Barry, B08 6BB. Duties included serving customers, stocking counter, stock taking, preparing window display.

### Hobbies and Interests

I have recently started to swim again and have joined a gym so as to keep fit and meet new people.

### References

Can be obtained from:

Mr C Bakewell,
Creamy Cakes UK,
Black Forest,
Bunwich,
CR3 4MY

# Business Plan for Claire's Cakes

## More questions

**How will the business run?** Sole Trader

**Does your business have any legal requirements?**
Yes

**Do you need to make any agreements?**
Yes - with customers and suppliers

**What health and safety issues affect your business?**
Kitchens inspected by health and safety executive

**What book-keeping system will you use?**
Euro Enterprise Evolutions Business Administration Toolkit

**Will you be registered for VAT?** No

**Will consumer legislation affect your business?**
Yes

**What insurance do you need for your business?**

Personal Liability Insurance, Car Insurance for Business, Equipment Insurance

# Business Plan for Claire's Cakes

## Questions to answer

**About the product**

Good quality cakes - fruit cakes, fancy sponges, range of gateaux, fruit pies, flans, cream cakes and speciality cakes (wedding, birthday etc).

Will supply individuals (party requirements) and local cafes/restaurants.

**Your customers**

Small restaurants and other commercial outlets, private clients

**What benefits are you offering your customers compared with your competitors?**

"Cakes like mother used to make".
5 star quality - High Street prices.
Speciality cakes - Tell me what you want and I will do it.

**Where will you work from?**

From home (very large kitchen with good range of cooking tools, large double oven, large chest freezer).

# Business Plan for Claire's Cakes

## Market Research

| **Claire's Cakes — Market Research** | | | | | | | | | |
|---|---|---|---|---|---|---|---|---|---|
| **I plan to start a business selling cakes. Please could you help by answering a few questions?** | | | | | | | | | |
| Which of the following would you be interested in buying? | | | | | | | | | **Total** |
| Home made cakes | 𝍸 | 𝍸 | 𝍸 | 𝍸 | 𝍸 | 𝍸 | 𝍸 | 𝍸 | **40** |
| Personalised Cakes | 𝍸 | 𝍸 | 𝍸 | 𝍸 | 𝍸 | 𝍸 | | | **30** |
| Speciality Cakes | 𝍸 | 𝍸 | | | | | | | **10** |
| What would you pay for homemade pies, fruit cakes or sponges? | | | | | | | | | **Total** |
| £2.00 | 𝍸 | 𝍸 | 𝍸 | 𝍸 | 𝍸 | 𝍸 | 𝍸 | 𝍸 | **40** |
| £3.00 | 𝍸 | 𝍸 | 𝍸 | 𝍸 | 𝍸 | 𝍸 | 𝍸 | 𝍸 | **40** |
| £4.00 | 𝍸 | 𝍸 | 𝍸 | 𝍸 | | | | | **20** |
| £5.00 | 𝍸 | 𝍸 | 𝍸 | 𝍸 | 𝍸 | | | | **25** |
| What would you pay for personalised or speciality cakes? | | | | | | | | | **Total** |
| £10.00 | 𝍸 | 𝍸 | 𝍸 | 𝍸 | 𝍸 | 𝍸 | 𝍸 | 𝍸 | **40** |
| £15.00 | 𝍸 | 𝍸 | 𝍸 | 𝍸 | 𝍸 | 𝍸 | 𝍸 | | **35** |
| £25.00 | 𝍸 | 𝍸 | 𝍸 | 𝍸 | | | | | **20** |
| £50.00 or more | 𝍸 | 𝍸 | 𝍸 | 𝍸 | 𝍸 | 𝍸 | 𝍸 | 𝍸 | **40** |

# Business Plan for Claire's Cakes

## Market Research

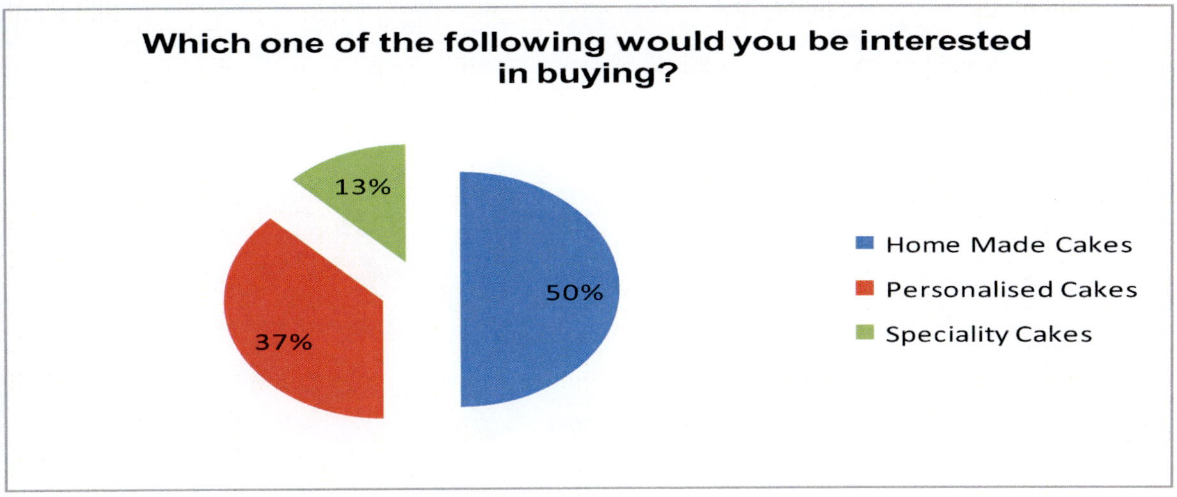

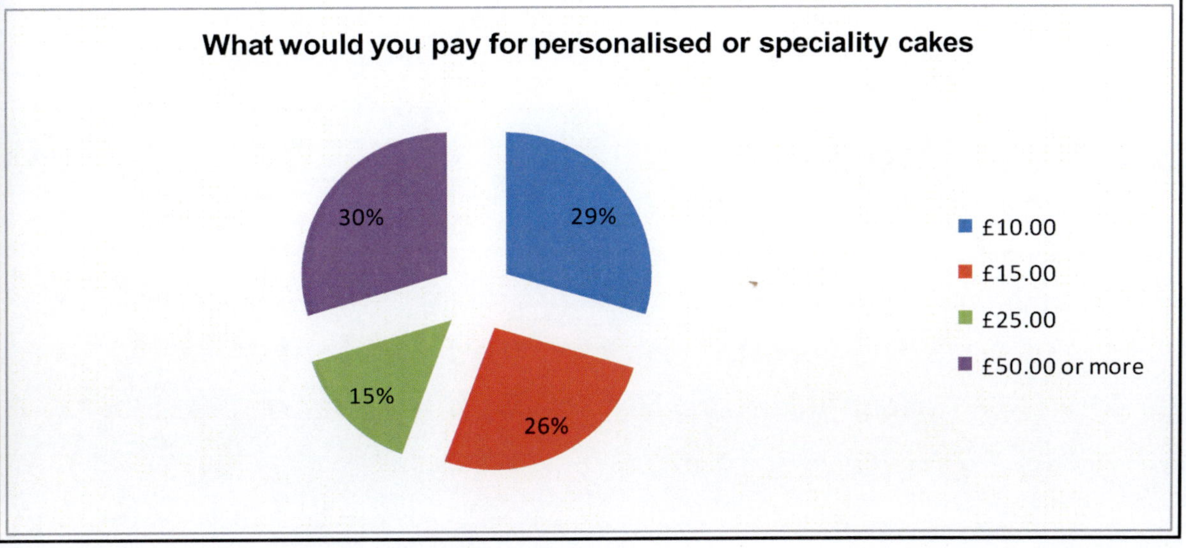

# Business Plan for Claire's Cakes

## Advertising

**113 Treacle Terrace**
**Battenberg**
**Swiss Cottage**
**SW9 99OZ**

**Telephone: 01284846209**
**Mobile: 07768263018**
**www.ccaps.co.uk**

# Claire's Cakes

**Cakes like Mother used to make?**
**Specialised Cakes**
**Fancy Cakes**
**Pastries**

**Discounts for orders over £100.00**

**Free delivery within 5 miles**

*Made to my recipe, made to yours,*
*How you like it—the choice is yours.*

# Business Plan for Claire's Cakes

## Customers, Competition and Suppliers

**Nearest competitors**

Chain cake shops: *Clotty Creams* and *Baking's*.
Supermarket *Freshdays*.

**Quality of competitors' goods**

*Clotty Creams* and *Baking's:* own brand cakes.
*Freshdays*: pre packed brand name cakes.

**How will your business supply a better product?**

Good home made, fresh, quality cakes.
"Cakes like mother used to make".
5 star quality—High Street prices.
Speciality cakes—Tell me what you want and I will do it.

**Who will be your suppliers?**

Local companies (letters of intent attached).

**Cost of competitors' goods?**

Visited outlets to compare prices:
Highest cost £50.00 for single layer iced fruit cake; my price £60.00.
Market research shows that people will pay my price for the personal touch.

# Business Plan for Claire's Cakes

## Letter to possible customer

***Claire's Cakes***
*113 Treacle Terrace*
*Battenberg*
*Swiss Cottage*
*SW9 99OZ*
*Tel: 01284846209*
*Mobile: 07768263018*
*www.ccaps.co.uk*

10th March 2007

John Coffee
Manager
Bistro Café
Smithson Road
Swiss Cottage
SW4 3OY

Dear Mr Coffee

I am setting up a cake making business. I can offer a wide range of home made style cakes and pastries that I feel would sell really well in your Bistro Café.

Please could you consider giving some time for a meeting to talk about the possibility of buying cakes from me.

I will telephone you within the next few days in the hope of making an appointment.

Yours sincerely

Claire Baker

Claire Baker

# Business Plan for Claire's Cakes

Letter from a possible customer

Bistro Café
Smithson Road
Swiss Cottage
SW 4 3OY
Tel 01287884209

3rd April 2007

Claire Baker
113 Treacle Terrace
Battenberg
Swiss Cottage
SW9 99OZ

Dear Mrs Baker

It was good to meet you. I would consider buying cakes and pastries from you when you start trading as long as your prices are competitive and that the quality remains high.

I wish you well with your business plans.

Yours sincerely

*John Coffee*

John Coffee
Manager, Bistro Café

# Business Plan for Claire's Cakes

Testimonial letter

Tulip Garden Centre
Marketplace Corner
Battenberg
Swiss Cottage
SW6 12ZO

21st March 2007

To whom it may concern

Re: Claire Baker of Claire's Cakes

Claire has supplied us with cakes and pastries for our weekend "homemade cake stall" for about two years now. Her products have always been of very good quality both in terms of taste and looks. They have been very popular with our customers, representing very good value for money.

Claire herself is a very pleasant lady who always delivers her orders in good time and takes care in packaging and presentation of the goods.

It has been a pleasure to be associated with her and we wish her well as she seeks to expand her business.

Yours faithfully

*Rosie Bud*

Rosie Bud

# Business Plan for Claire's Cakes

Letter to possible supplier

***Claire's Cakes***
*113 Treacle Terrace*
*Battenberg*
*Swiss Cottage SW9 99OZ*
*Tel: 01284846209*
*Mobile: 07768263018*
*www.ccaps.co.uk*

10th March 2007

Sweetland Wholesalers
Cherry Orchard Retail Park
Swiss Cottage
SW9 17OX

Dear Sirs

I am looking into where to buy supplies for my cake making business.

Please could you send me any information on your products with prices, discounts and terms of payment.

I look forward to hearing from you.

Yours sincerely

Claire Baker

Claire Baker

# Business Plan for Claire's Cakes

## Financial Assumptions

| Claire's Cakes Financial Assumptions | | | | | | |
|---|---|---|---|---|---|---|
| Sales and Purchases - Cash Sales | | | | | | |
| Month | No of weeks per month<br>A | No of sales per week<br>B | Selling price per unit<br>C | Total Sales<br>A x B x C | Purchase price per unit<br>D | Total purchases<br>A x B x D |
| 1 | 4 | 4 | 55.00 | 880.00 | 10.00 | 160.00 |
| 2 | 4 | 4 | 55.00 | 880.00 | 10.00 | 160.00 |
| 3 | 5 | 3 | 45.00 | 675.00 | 6.00 | 90.00 |
| 4 | 4 | 3 | 45.00 | 540.00 | 6.00 | 72.00 |
| 5 | 4 | 2 | 30.00 | 240.00 | 5.00 | 40.00 |
| 6 | 5 | 6 | 30.00 | 900.00 | 5.00 | 150.00 |
| 7 | 4 | 6 | 30.00 | 720.00 | 5.00 | 120.00 |
| 8 | 4 | 2 | 30.00 | 240.00 | 5.00 | 40.00 |
| 9 | 5 | 3 | 30.00 | 450.00 | 5.00 | 75.00 |
| 10 | 4 | 4 | 45.00 | 720.00 | 6.00 | 96.00 |
| 11 | 4 | 6 | 30.00 | 720.00 | 5.00 | 120.00 |
| 12 | 5 | 4 | 30.00 | 600.00 | 5.00 | 100.00 |
| Total | 52 | | | 7565.00 | | 1223.00 |

# Business Plan for Claire's Cakes

## Financial Assumptions

| Claire's Cakes Financial Assumptions | | | | | | |
|---|---|---|---|---|---|---|
| Sales and Purchases - Credit Sales | | | | | | |
| Month | No of weeks per month<br>A | No of sales per week<br>B | Selling price per unit<br>C | Total Sales<br>A x B x C | Purchase price per unit<br>D | Total purchases<br>A x B x D |
| 1 | 4 | 54 | 5.00 | 1080.00 | 2.00 | 432.00 |
| 2 | 4 | 60 | 5.00 | 1200.00 | 2.00 | 480.00 |
| 3 | 5 | 60 | 5.00 | 1500.00 | 2.00 | 600.00 |
| 4 | 4 | 54 | 5.00 | 1080.00 | 2.00 | 432.00 |
| 5 | 4 | 54 | 5.00 | 1080.00 | 2.00 | 432.00 |
| 6 | 5 | 54 | 5.00 | 1350.00 | 2.00 | 540.00 |
| 7 | 4 | 60 | 5.00 | 1200.00 | 2.00 | 480.00 |
| 8 | 4 | 54 | 5.00 | 1080.00 | 2.00 | 432.00 |
| 9 | 5 | 54 | 5.00 | 1350.00 | 2.00 | 540.00 |
| 10 | 4 | 54 | 5.00 | 1080.00 | 2.00 | 432.00 |
| 11 | 4 | 54 | 5.00 | 1080.00 | 2.00 | 432.00 |
| 12 | 5 | 54 | 5.00 | 1350.00 | 2.00 | 540.00 |
| Total | 52 | | | 14430.00 | | 5772.00 |

# Business Plan for Claire's Cakes

## Cash Flow Forecast

| Number of Weeks | | 4 | 4 | 5 | 4 | 4 |
|---|---|---|---|---|---|---|
| **Month** | **Start Up** | **1** | **2** | **3** | **4** | **5** |
| Cash Sales | | 880.00 | 880.00 | 675.00 | 540.00 | 240.00 |
| Credit Sales | | | | 1080.00 | 1200.00 | 1500.00 |
| Bank Loan | 1000.00 | | | | | |
| Loan (family/ friends) | 1000.00 | | | | | |
| Grant | 1000.00 | | | | | |
| Cash Introduced | 1000.00 | | | | | |
| **Total Receipts (A)** | 4000.00 | 880.00 | 880.00 | 1755.00 | 1740.00 | 1740.00 |
| | | | | | | |
| Business Stock | 150.00 | 592.00 | 640.00 | 690.00 | 504.00 | 472.00 |
| Drawings | | 800.00 | 800.00 | 800.00 | 800.00 | 800.00 |
| Telephone | 50.00 | 30.00 | 30.00 | 30.00 | 30.00 | 30.00 |
| Stationery & Postage | 150.00 | 10.00 | 10.00 | 10.00 | 10.00 | 10.00 |
| Travel & Motor | | 40.00 | 40.00 | 40.00 | 40.00 | 40.00 |
| Repairs & Maintenance | | | | | | |
| Heating & lighting | | 25.00 | 25.00 | 25.00 | 25.00 | 25.00 |
| Rent & Rates | | 50.00 | 50.00 | 50.00 | 50.00 | 50.00 |
| Loan repayments | | | | 20.00 | 20.00 | 20.00 |
| **Total Payments (B)** | 350.00 | 1547.00 | 1595.00 | 1665.00 | 1479.00 | 1447.00 |
| **A - B** | 3650.00 | -667.00 | -715.00 | 90.00 | 261.00 | 293.00 |
| **Opening Balance** | 0.00 | 3650.00 | 2983.00 | 2268.00 | 2358.00 | 2619.00 |
| **Closing Balance** | 3650.00 | 2983.00 | 2268.00 | 2358.00 | 2619.00 | 2912.00 |

# Business Plan for Claire's Cakes

## Cash Flow Forecast

| | | | | | | | |
|---|---|---|---|---|---|---|---|
| **5** | **4** | **4** | **5** | **4** | **4** | **5** | **Totals** |
| **6** | **7** | **8** | **9** | **10** | **11** | **12** | |
| 900.00 | 720.00 | 240.00 | 450.00 | 720.00 | 720.00 | 600.00 | 7565.00 |
| 1080.00 | 1080.00 | 1350.00 | 1200.00 | 1080.00 | 1350.00 | 1080.00 | 12000.00 |
| | | | | | | | 1000.00 |
| | | | | | | | 1000.00 |
| | | | | | | | 1000.00 |
| | | | | | | | 1000.00 |
| 1980.00 | 1800.00 | 1590.00 | 1650.00 | 1800.00 | 2070.00 | 1680.00 | 23565.00 |
| | | | | | | | |
| 690.00 | 600.00 | 472.00 | 615.00 | 528.00 | 552.00 | 640.00 | 7145.00 |
| 800.00 | 800.00 | 800.00 | 800.00 | 800.00 | 800.00 | 800.00 | 9600.00 |
| 30.00 | 30.00 | 30.00 | 30.00 | 30.00 | 30.00 | 30.00 | 410.00 |
| 10.00 | 10.00 | 10.00 | 10.00 | 10.00 | 10.00 | 10.00 | 270.00 |
| 40.00 | 40.00 | 40.00 | 40.00 | 40.00 | 40.00 | 40.00 | 480.00 |
| | | | | | | | |
| 25.00 | 25.00 | 25.00 | 25.00 | 25.00 | 25.00 | 25.00 | 300.00 |
| 50.00 | 50.00 | 50.00 | 50.00 | 50.00 | 50.00 | 50.00 | 600.00 |
| 20.00 | 20.00 | 20.00 | 20.00 | 20.00 | 20.00 | 20.00 | 200.00 |
| 1665.00 | 1575.00 | 1447.00 | 1590.00 | 1503.00 | 1527.00 | 1615.00 | 19005.00 |
| 315.00 | 225.00 | 143.00 | 60.00 | 297.00 | 543.00 | 65.00 | 4560.00 |
| 2912.00 | 3452.00 | 3452.00 | 3595.00 | 3655.00 | 3952.00 | 4495.00 | 000.00 |
| 3227.00 | 352.00 | 3595.00 | 3655.00 | 3952.00 | 4495.00 | 4560.00 | 000.00 |

# Business Plan for Claire's Cakes

## Break even

My break even point comes in month 3 when

- Total receipts are £1755.00 and
- Total payments are £1665.00

# Business Plan for Claire's Cakes

## S.W.O.T. Analysis

| | |
|---|---|
| **Strengths** | I am hard working, well organised and am in good health. I am a good cook with a lot of experience and have good contacts in the catering trade |
| **Weaknesses** | If I am ill or go on holiday |
| **Opportunities** | There is definitely a market for my product. The Internet will give me the chance to develop the speciality cakes side of the business. There may be an opportunity to open my own shop or go into a partnership. |
| **Threats** | Competition from supermarkets and chain bakeries. Possible complaints from neighbours. Health and safety issues. |

# Business Plan for Claire's Cakes

## Contingency Plan

If I cannot deliver because of illness or car problems members of my family will make the deliveries

If I cannot produce new stock because of illness I will have some frozen products in hand to supply customers for a few days.

If I cannot produce new stock because of equipment breakdown I have an arrangement with my catering equipment provider to replace or repair my equipment within a 24 hour period.

## Now you have seen the business plan for Claire's Cakes it's time to see how to do your business plan

**I will help you to do your plan step by step.**

**The 3 parts of the Business Plan are:**



Find out more ... GO



**In this part you will find samples of cheques, invoices, business cards etc and other useful stuff!**

# Me and My Business

## Part 1 of your Business Plan

# Things you need to know

## Why do a Business Plan?

You will need to do a Business Plan if:

- You want to get a loan
- You want to get a grant

The Plan will show who ever is going to lend or give you money that you have done some work on your business idea.

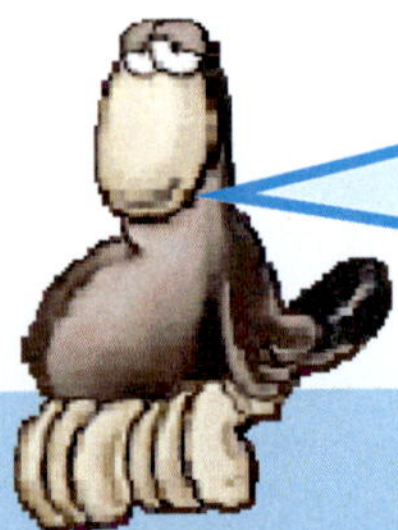

**The plan will also help you see if your idea will work**

Doing the Plan will help you think about things like

- Skills you have
- Prices customers will pay
- How much to charge
- How much you need to live on
- If the business will make money
- How to run the business

# Things you need to know

## Start up

**The money you start your business with is called**

**Start up**

- You may have money of your own (e.g. savings)
- You may have money from family or friends
- You may get a loan
- You may get a grant

**Remember!**

**You will need to open a bank account just for your business**

**You will need to have a business name for your account**

# Things you need to know

## Product or Service?

**This page is to help you think about what your business will sell — Product or Service**

**A business may sell things (products)**
**e.g. food, toys**

Will you be making something (**product**) to sell?

Will you buy something (**product**) to sell to someone else?

Will you be selling your **product** from home?

Will you be selling your **product** from another place (such as a shop)?

**Some businesses give a service**
**e.g. hairdressing, window cleaning**

Will you be providing a **service**?

Will you be providing a **service** from home?

Will you be providing a **service** in other people's homes (e.g. cleaning or decorating)?

Will you need a car to provide the **service**?

# Things you need to know

## Your product or your service

You need to tell your funder (this may be a bank) about your **product** or your **service**

Does the **product** look good?

Is it attractively packaged?

Do you find out what your customer needs or wants?

Do you deliver the **service** on time?

Do you clean up after each job?

So how good is it?

Do you give helpful advice?

Do you make every customer feel important?

**You need to give your loan provider a positive statement e.g.**

**I offer a good product / service that will meet my customers' needs.**

# Things you need to know

## What Sort of Business—how will you trade?

*There are three main ways to run a business — as a:*

### Sole Trader

You can start this sort of business at once. A sole trader is responsible for the money the business owes.

### Partnership

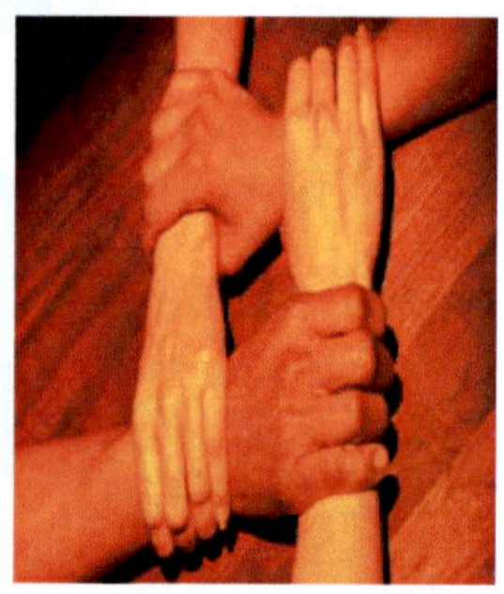

Two or more people running a business together. Each partner is responsible for the total money the business owes.

### Limited Company

Can cost a lot to set up but keeps business assets separate from personal assets.
You need help from solicitor or accountant to set up a limited company.
[Assets = what you or your business owns (e.g. savings, house, stock)

# Things you need to know

## S.W.O.T.

| | | | |
|---|---|---|---|
| **S**trengths | = | What I am good at |  |
| **W**eaknesses | = | What I am not so good at! |  |
| **O**pportunities | = | What will help my business |  |
| **T**hreats | = | What might harm my business |  |

**Doing a S.W.O.T. analysis will help you run your business.**

It will help you for example to:

- make the best use of your strengths
- think about what you will do about your weaknesses
- look for ways to make your business grow
- think about how to deal with problems that may stop your business growing

# Things you need to know

## What if …?

You will need to think of a back-up plan to help you if something does go wrong that will make it hard for you to go on with your business.

This is called a **contingency plan.**

The sort of things to think about are :

What you will do if ...

- Your car breaks down
- You are ill
- Bad weather stops you working
- Tools or equipment break down
- A supplier lets you down

## It is important to think about this!

**Follow Business Birdie**
**Take the steps**
**To make your CV**
**A step to success**

A CV is made up of 7 parts

1. **Personal Details**
2. **Personal Profile**
3. **Skills and Training**
4. **Work History**
5. **Voluntary Work**
6. **Hobbies and Interests**
7. **References**

Look at the CV for Steve of Ever Shine Windows to give you the idea.

Next page GO

| | |
|---|---|
| **Name** | Steven Samuel Quiggy |
| **Address** | 54 Rinse Road<br>Sudingham |
| **Post Code** | B88 8LE |
| **Telephone No.** | 017965845 |
| **Mobile No.** | 077936821 |
| **Email** | quiggyss@wanado.com |
| **Driving Licence** | Clean (no points) licence |

**Personal Profile**

I am reliable and willing to work hard. I enjoy working out of doors and have already had experience at cleaning windows with an agency. I have worked more recently as cleaning supervisor for a local supermarket where it was my job to check stock and order cleaning supplies. It was also my job to give out tasks to my team and to timetable these tasks to fit in with the day to day running of the supermarket. I believe the skills learned will help me to run a profitable window cleaning business.

**Skills/Training**

On the job training in using cleaning products and tools, customer care, record -keeping. Training in health and safety, storage of cleaning products

**January 2006**

Health and Safety Certificate

**CV S. S. Quiggy (page 2)**

**Work History**

**July 2001-August 2007 Cleaning Supervisor**

**Brightshine Cleaning Agency**, Bubbles Lane, Sudingham, B89 6BL

Duties included checking rotas, equipment/supplies, working as team leader, customer care.

**May 1998-June 2001 Cleaning Technician**

**Wellbright Shop Cleaning Company,** Shining Road, Sudingham B90 9SR
Duties included checking and ordering stock, window cleaning.

**Voluntary Work**

**West Endon Adult Training Centre,** Central Road, Sudingham B94 8CR

Duties include helping to take groups on walks/trips.

**Hobbies and Interests**

I like coarse fishing and do competitions. I keep records for my team.

**References**

References can be obtained if needed.

# CV

A CV is an outline of your life story

You may need to put a CV into your business plan.

**Pages 34 - 47 show you how to do the 7 parts that make up a CV**

### *Useful Tips*

- Put what fits with the work you want to do
- Check that what you put is correct
- Check your spelling
- Keep it short - 2 pages

It is best to do your final CV on a computer - it looks better and uses less space.

Look out for computer tips!

Your turn to write

**Start with the easy bit**

# CV

## 1. Personal Details

Copy

**Name** ..........................................................................

**Address** ..........................................................................

..........................................................................

**Post Code** ..........................................................................

**Tel. No.** ..........................................................................

**Mobile No.** ..........................................................................

**Email** ..........................................................................

**Driving Licence** ..........................................................................
**(if yes, what type)**

**Have a look at the next page for tips to make this look good on computer**

# CV

## 1. Personal Details

Your computer screen may not look like this one but the tools are the same

Use a clear font e.g.

Arial font size 12

Type headings in Bold

To get Bold, click on B

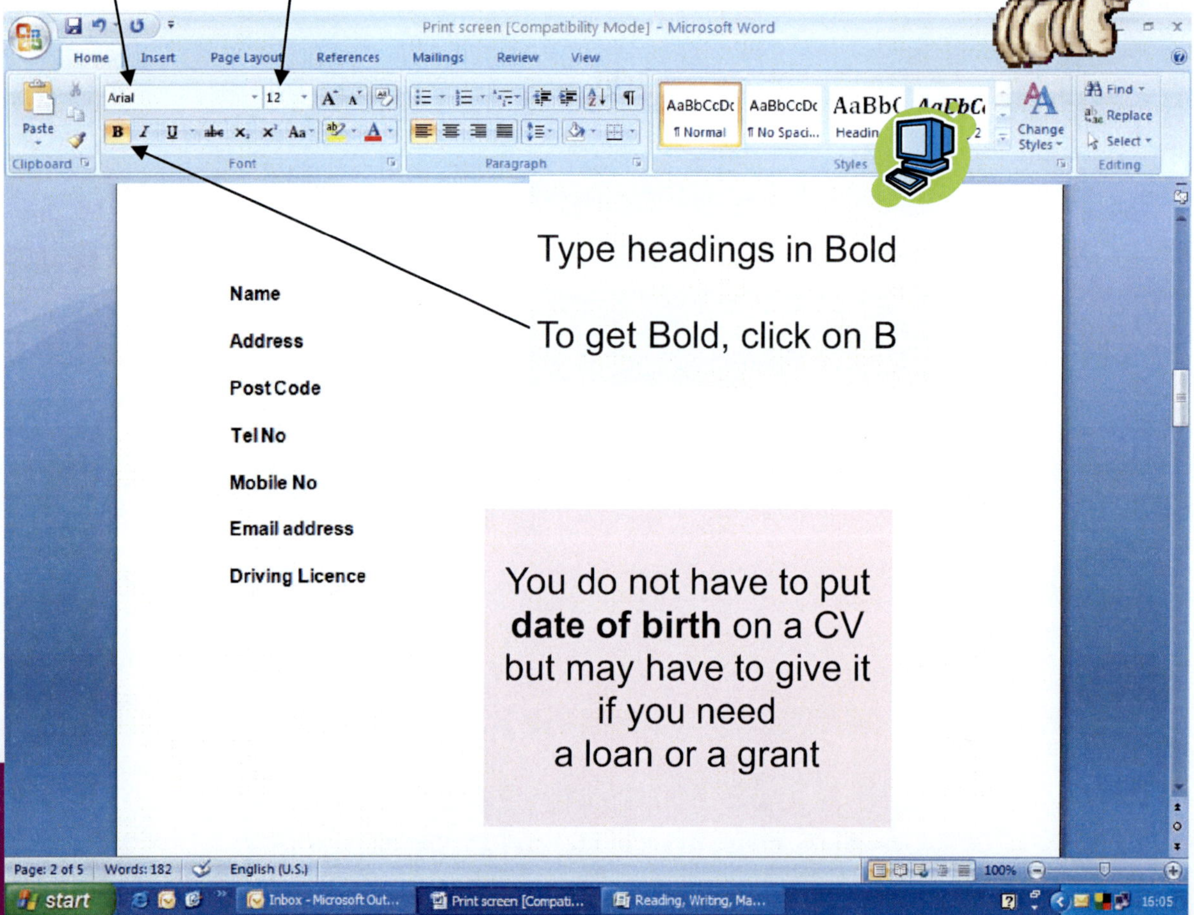


You do not have to put **date of birth** on a CV but may have to give it if you need a loan or a grant

# CV

## 1. Personal Details

You need to give your CV a title on the computer
e.g. Steve's CV 2007

***Useful tip***

Do save your CV as you go along!

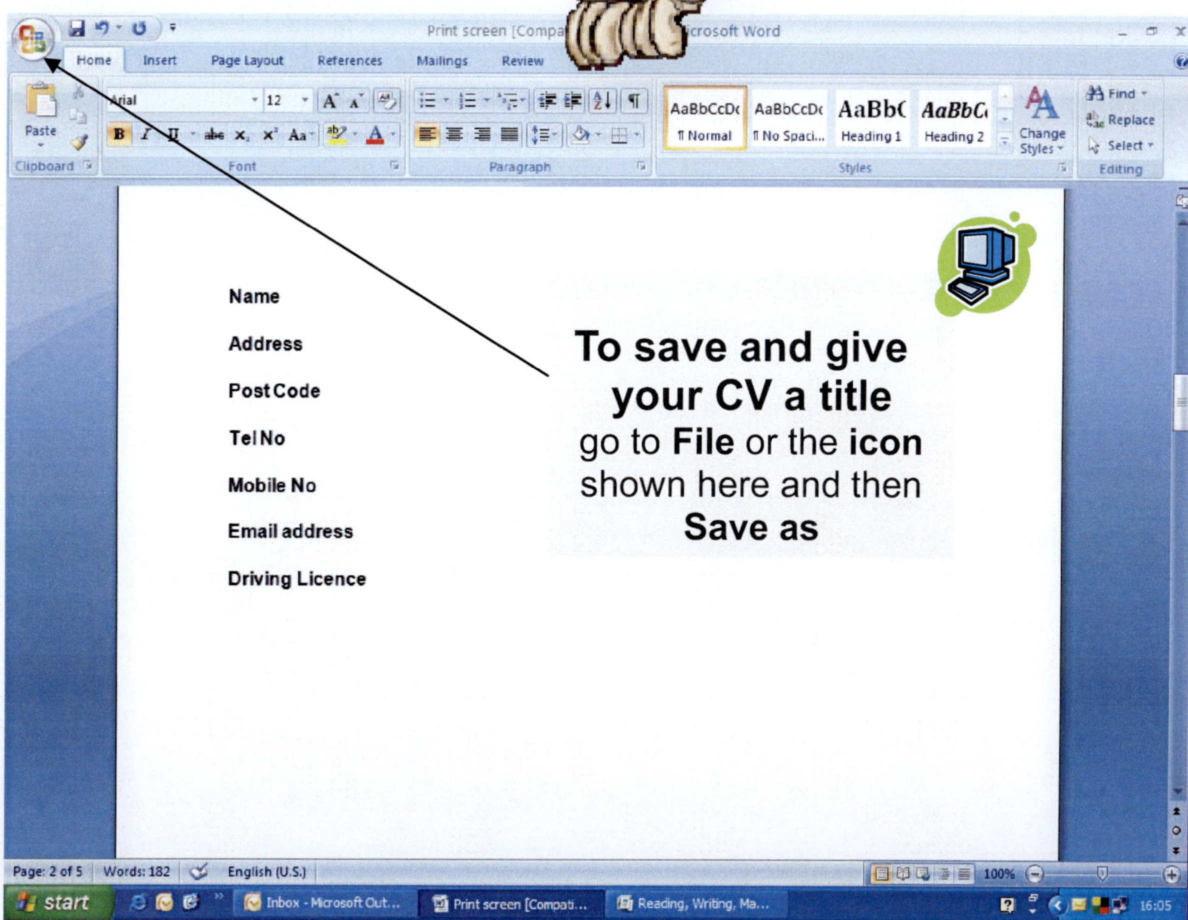


**To save and give your CV a title**
go to **File** or the **icon** shown here and then **Save as**

# CV

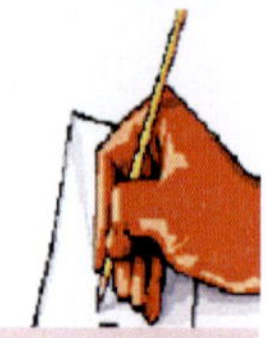

## 2. Personal Profile

Copy

The **Personal Profile** is about you. Think about ...

- What I am good at (Strengths)
- What I hope to go on to do (Goals)

*Example 1:* I am honest, punctual, trustworthy and hardworking and get on well with people. I have good hairdressing skills that I want to use in a mobile hairdressing business.

*Example 2:* I am a reliable, energetic person. I have spent ten years in the retail trade and have worked my way up to shop manager. I have learned a lot about good marketing practice and customer care and believe I can make a success of my business.

**Write your Personal Profile here**

..................................................................................................

..................................................................................................

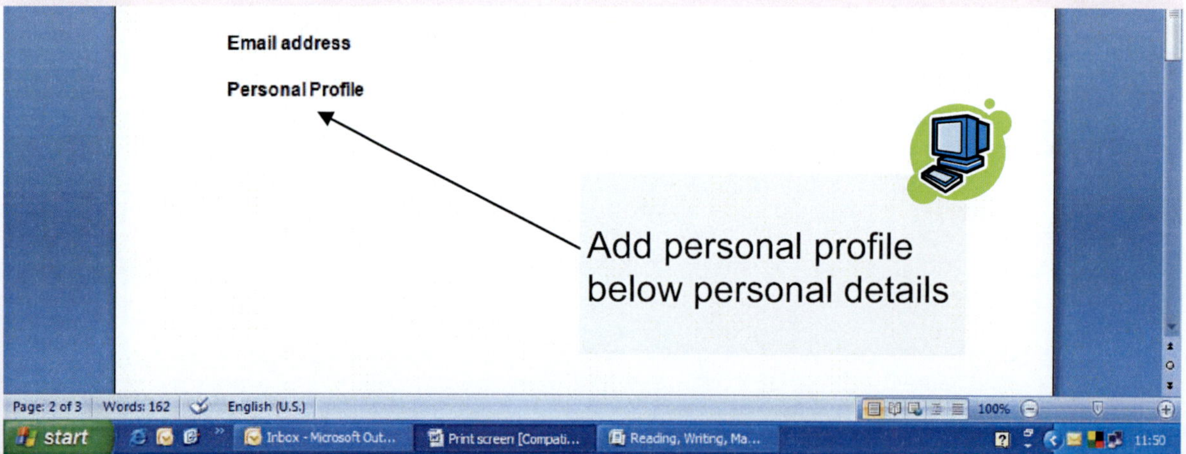

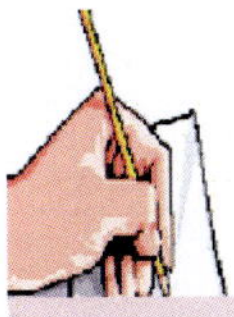

# CV

## 3. Training and Skills

To start up a business you need to have the skills to match.

**Think about any training and skills that fit your business. This can be:**

- **Awards** (e.g. from school/college)
- **Skills training** (e.g. college, training centre course)

- **Skills learned on the job**

**Steve of Ever Shine Window Cleaners has picked up skills from the jobs he has done**

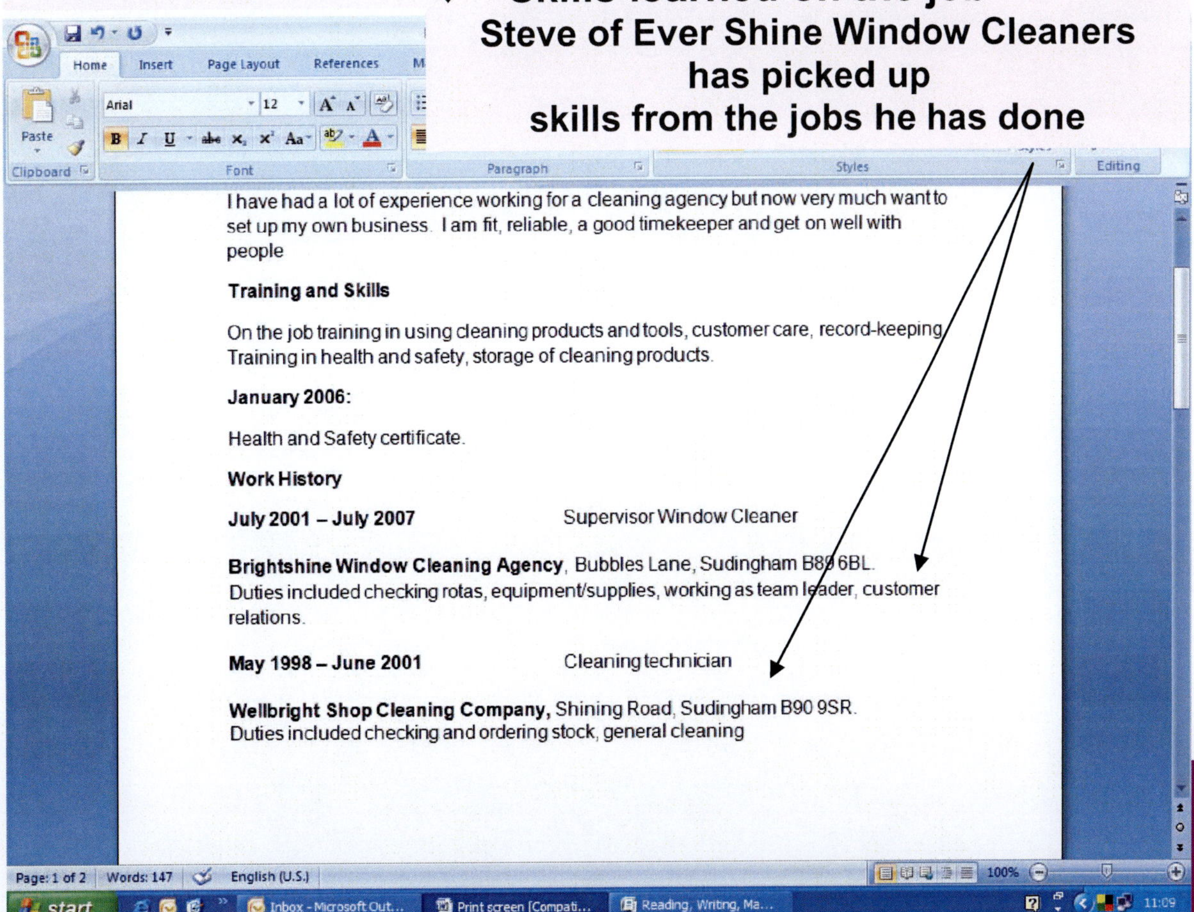
I have had a lot of experience working for a cleaning agency but now very much want to set up my own business. I am fit, reliable, a good timekeeper and get on well with people

**Training and Skills**

On the job training in using cleaning products and tools, customer care, record-keeping. Training in health and safety, storage of cleaning products.

**January 2006:**

Health and Safety certificate.

**Work History**

**July 2001 – July 2007** Supervisor Window Cleaner

**Brightshine Window Cleaning Agency**, Bubbles Lane, Sudingham B89 6BL. Duties included checking rotas, equipment/supplies, working as team leader, customer relations.

**May 1998 – June 2001** Cleaning technician

**Wellbright Shop Cleaning Company,** Shining Road, Sudingham B90 9SR. Duties included checking and ordering stock, general cleaning

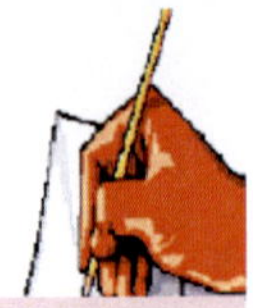

# CV

## 3. Training/Skills

The next few pages are to help you think about training, skills and qualities

- Don't worry if you do not have awards for training.
- Think about the skills that will help you run your business.

**To help get you started here are some skills and qualities needed to set up a window cleaning business:**

**Skills**

- Being able to drive
- Good at keeping customer/payment records
- Able to handle ladders etc

**Qualities**

- Good level of fitness
- Reliable
- Good with people

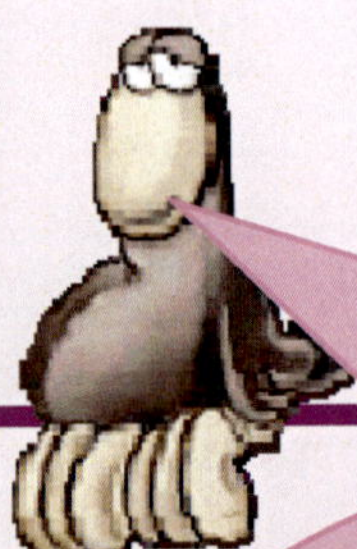

**Qualities** are about you as a person e.g.

- good timekeeper
- get on well with people

**These go under Personal Profile**

# CV

## 3. Training/Skills

Copy

| Skills I have |
| --- |
| |
| |
| |
| |
| |
| |

# CV

## 3. Training/Skills

Copy

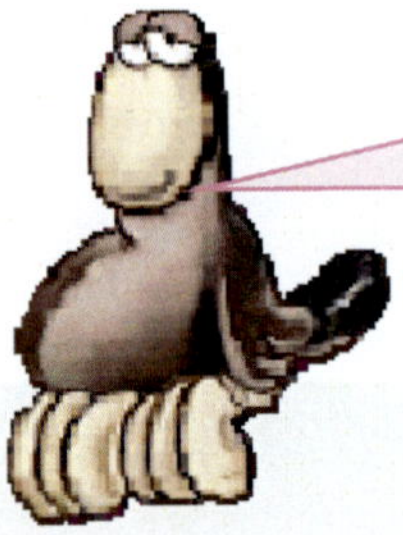

Write down any training you have had that will help you run your business.

This can be on the job training or a course you have done

Put down the **date** you got your award e.g.

- June 2007 Health and Safety Certificate
- April 2006 Health and Hygiene Certificate

# CV

## 3. Training/Skills

**Qualities**
(such as being reliable)
go under
**Personal Profile**.

**Skills learned on the job**
go under
**Training and Skills**

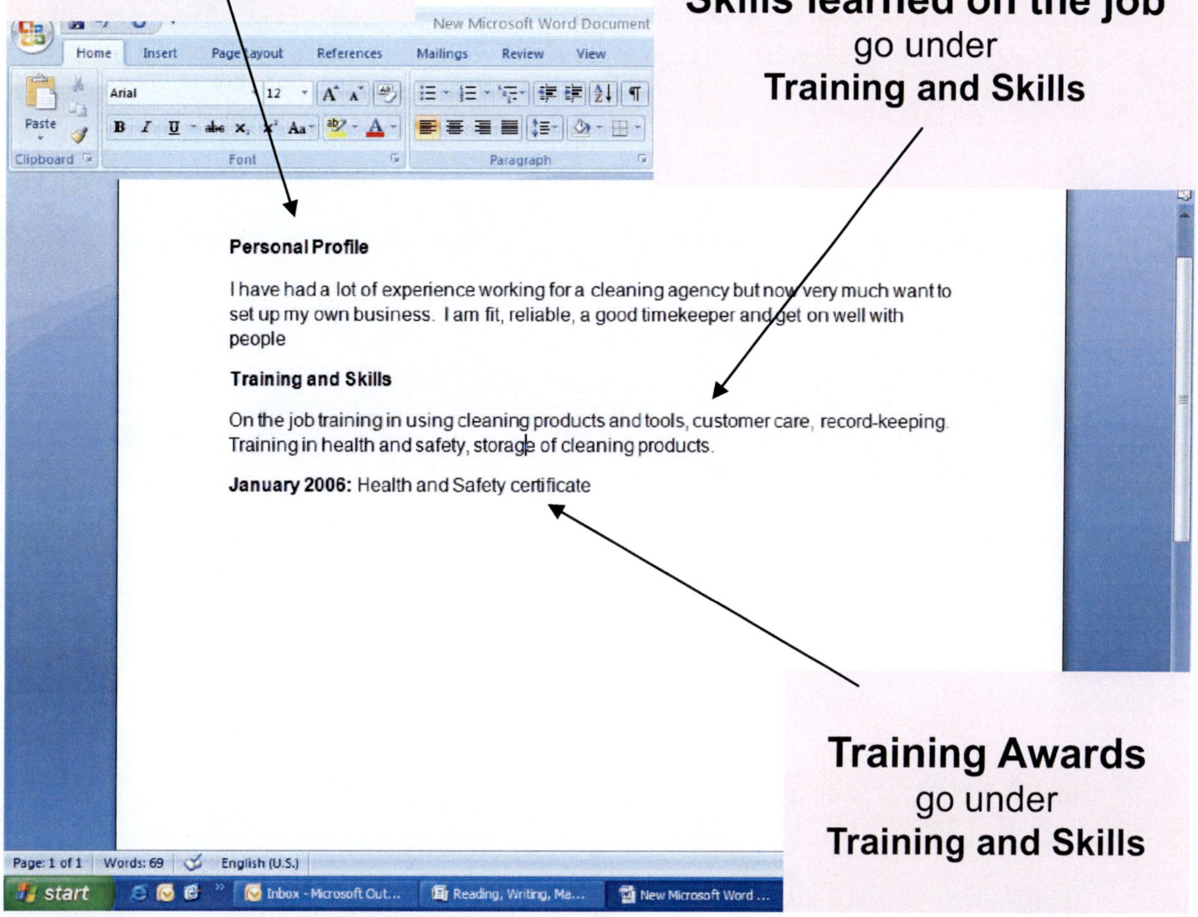


**Training Awards**
go under
**Training and Skills**

**Awards can be**

- **NVQ's**
- **work based awards**

# CV

## 4. Work History

This is about jobs you have had

- Put down the jobs that fit the business you want to do
- Put down work that shows you have the skills you need for your business

**Voluntary work for an Organisation**

You may not have had many paid jobs but you may have done work for someone else without pay. This is called voluntary work and can be:

- Gardening
- Taking telephone calls
- Painting
- Mending things
- Working in a charity shop

### For Work History and Voluntary Work

- Put the dates you have had jobs - start with your last job and work back
- Put the name of the company you worked for
- Put the name of your job (job title)
- List what you had to do (duties)

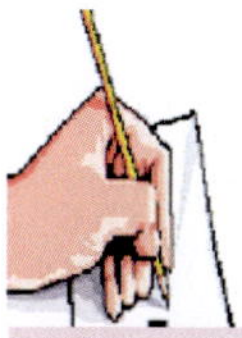

# CV

## 4. Work History

Copy ✓

**Work History**
goes after
**Training and Skills**

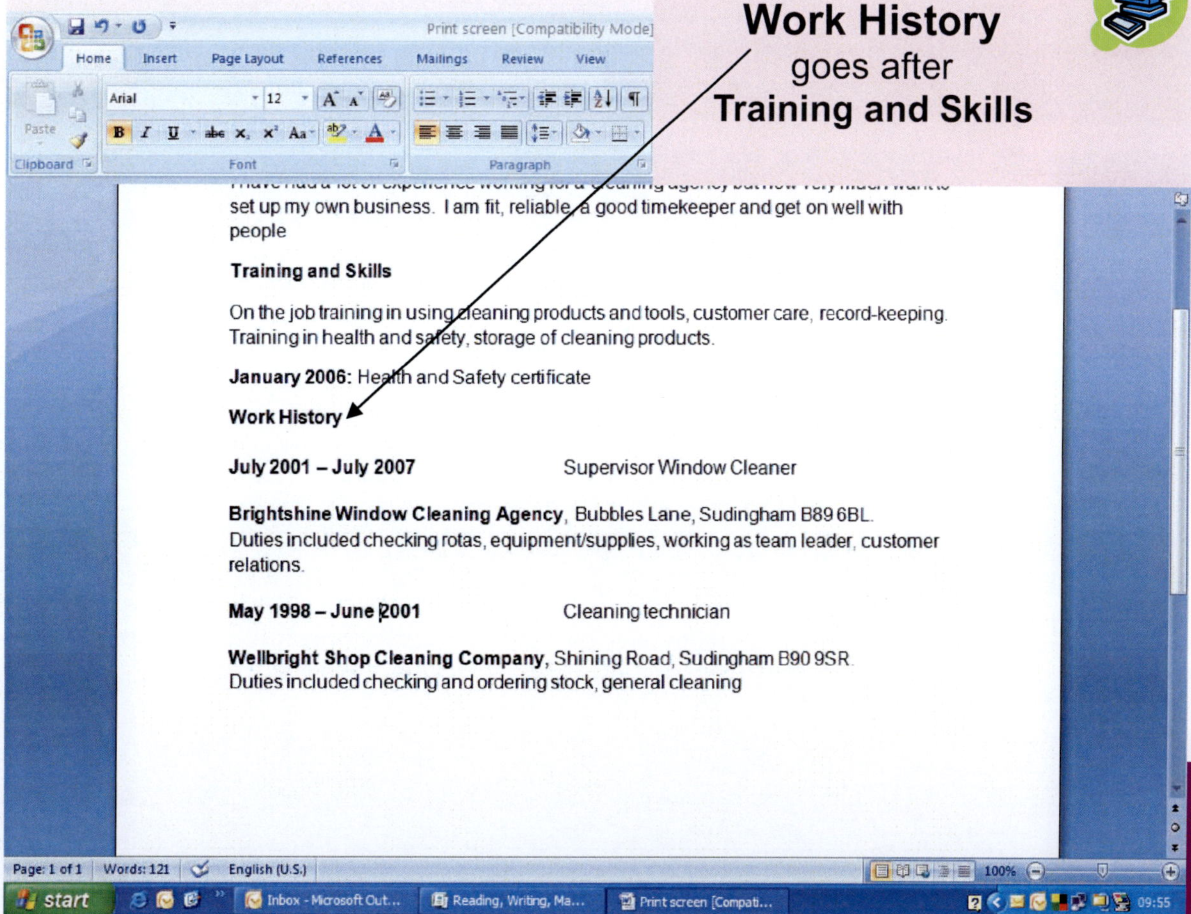


set up my own business. I am fit, reliable, a good timekeeper and get on well with people

**Training and Skills**

On the job training in using cleaning products and tools, customer care, record-keeping. Training in health and safety, storage of cleaning products.

**January 2006:** Health and Safety certificate

**Work History**

**July 2001 – July 2007** Supervisor Window Cleaner

**Brightshine Window Cleaning Agency**, Bubbles Lane, Sudingham B89 6BL. Duties included checking rotas, equipment/supplies, working as team leader, customer relations.

**May 1998 – June 2001** Cleaning technician

**Wellbright Shop Cleaning Company**, Shining Road, Sudingham B90 9SR. Duties included checking and ordering stock, general cleaning

# CV

## 5. Voluntary Work

Copy ✓

.......................................................................

.......................................................................

.......................................................................

.......................................................................

.......................................................................

.......................................................................

**Voluntary Work**
goes after
**Work History**

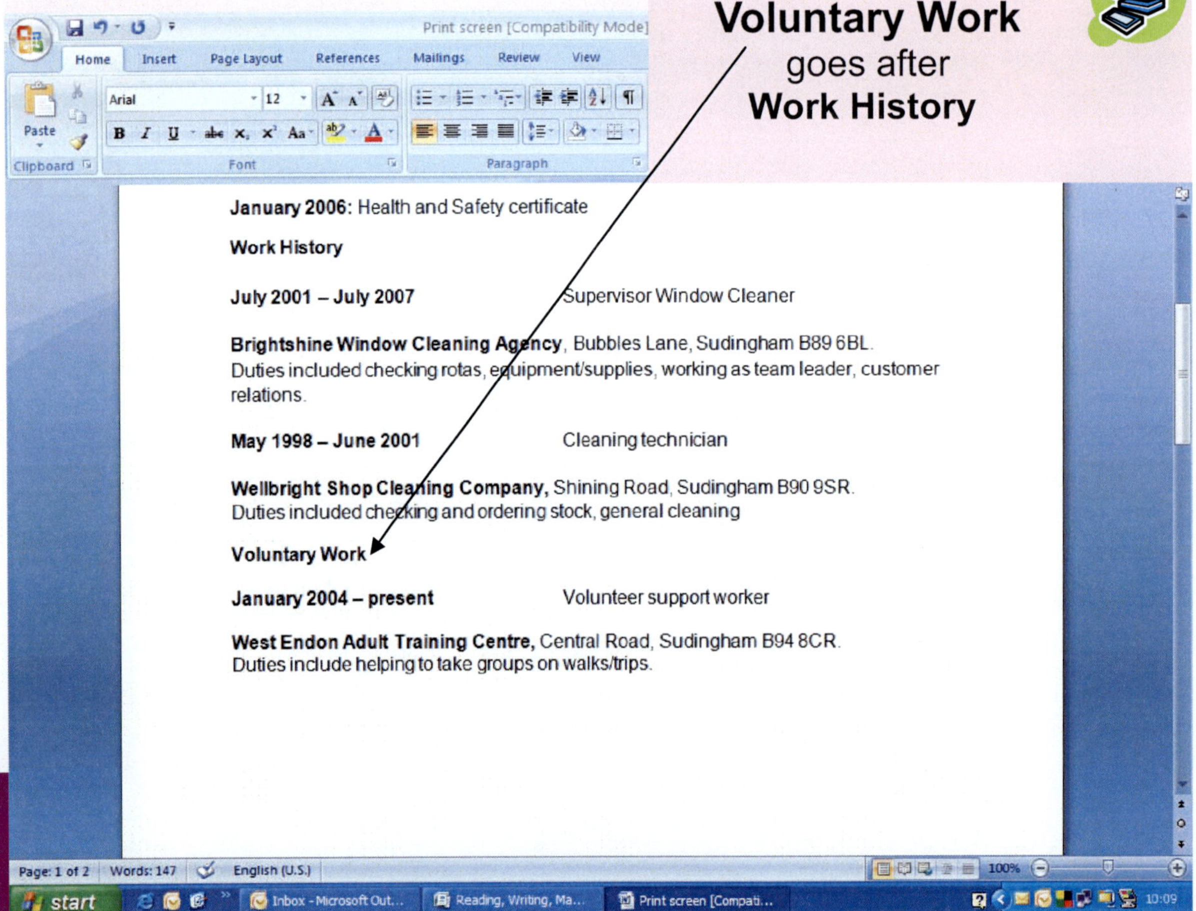

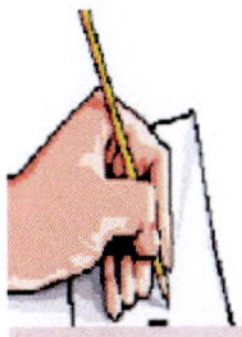

# Skills and Training in a CV

## 6. Hobbies and Interests

Copy

Write about what you like to do in your spare time.

- Do not just do a list but write a bit about your hobby.
- Here are some examples to help you but not to copy!

*Example 1:* **I like coarse fishing and do competitions. I keep the records for my team.**

*Example 3:* **I enjoy cooking and have been to classes for making and decorating cakes.**

You may have a hobby or interest that shows you have the skills you need in your business

**Hobbies and Interests**

..............................................................................................

..............................................................................................

..............................................................................................

# CV

## 6. Hobbies and Interests

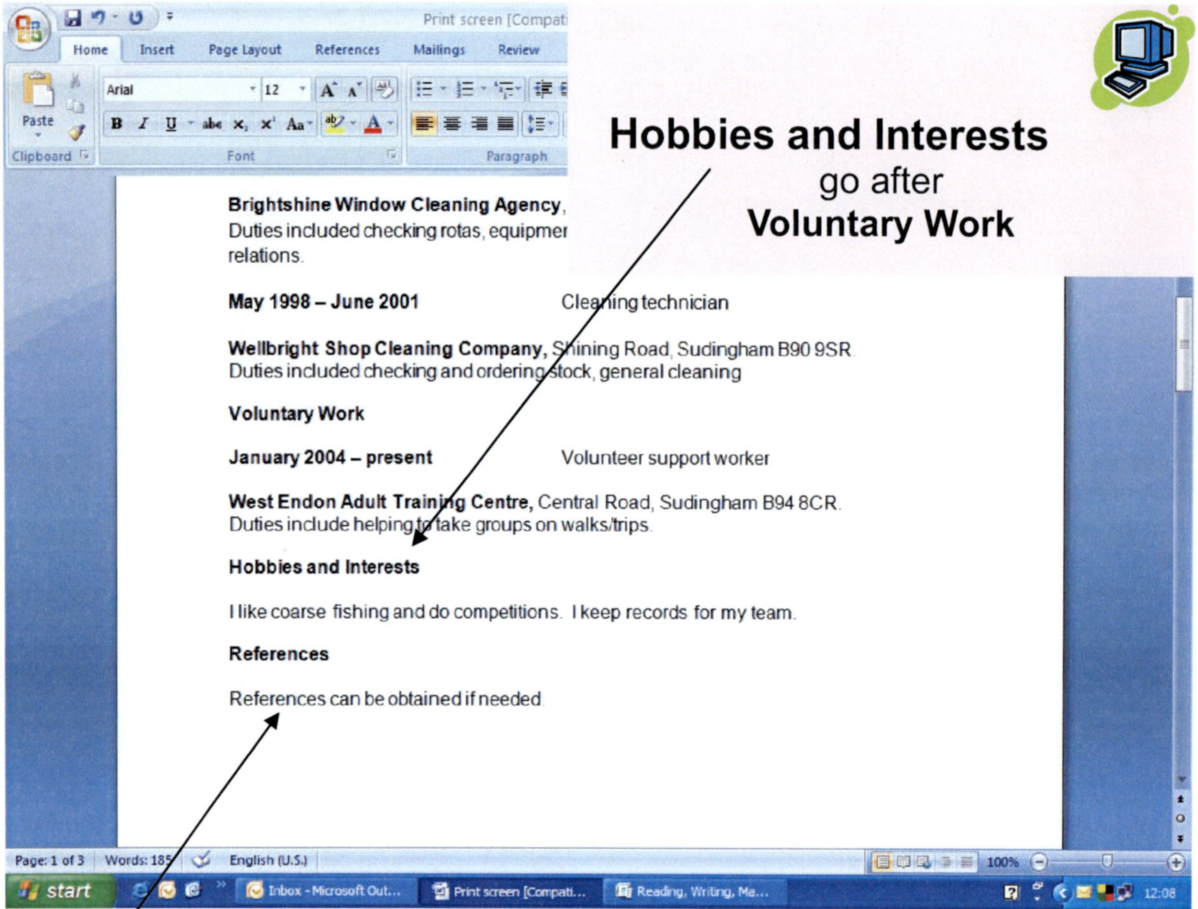

**Brightshine Window Cleaning Agency,**
Duties included checking rotas, equipmen
relations.

**May 1998 – June 2001** Cleaning technician

**Wellbright Shop Cleaning Company,** Shining Road, Sudingham B90 9SR
Duties included checking and ordering stock, general cleaning

**Voluntary Work**

**January 2004 – present** Volunteer support worker

**West Endon Adult Training Centre,** Central Road, Sudingham B94 8CR
Duties include helping to take groups on walks/trips.

**Hobbies and Interests**

I like coarse fishing and do competitions. I keep records for my team.

**References**

References can be obtained if needed.

**Hobbies and Interests**
go after
**Voluntary Work**

## References

- A **reference** is a letter written about you by another person
- This could be: teacher, tutor, manager or someone who has known you for two years or more.
- The name and address of a referee goes at the end of your CV **or** you can put ***References can be obtained if needed***

**If you do not have a computer you may wish to fill in the blank CV form on the next page and ask someone else to put it on computer for you.**

GO

# CV

## CV Template

Copy

**Name** ..............................................................................

**Address** ..............................................................................

..............................................................................

**Post Code** ..............................................................................

**Tel. No.** ..............................................................................

**Mobile No.** ..............................................................................

**Driving Licence** ..............................................................................

**Personal Profile**

..........................................................................................................

..........................................................................................................

..........................................................................................................

..........................................................................................................

**Skills/Training**

..........................................................................................................

..........................................................................................................

..........................................................................................................

..........................................................................................................

..........................................................................................................

..........................................................................................................

# CV

## CV Template

Copy

**Work History**

........................................................................................................

........................................................................................................

........................................................................................................

........................................................................................................

........................................................................................................

........................................................................................................

........................................................................................................

........................................................................................................

**Hobbies and Interests**

........................................................................................................

........................................................................................................

........................................................................................................

........................................................................................................

........................................................................................................

**References**

........................................................................................................

........................................................................................................

........................................................................................................

........................................................................................................

# Market Research

## Part 2 of your Business Plan

Who will buy my services?

Where can I sell my goods?

Will my goods sell well?

Where can I get help from?

How much will my services cost?

Where can I find a supplier?

How will I find out about my market?

How do I know what price to ask!!!!!!!!

# Market Research

## Why do Market Research?

You need to be able to prove that people will want to buy what you have to sell.

*If you start a business and no one wants to buy from you there will be no business!*

## *Market Research is a must!*

**Talk to people you know about your idea**

- Do they want to buy what you are offering?
- How much will they pay?
- Find out what they think
- Do they have ideas that will make your business better?
- Make notes about what they say

# Market Research

## What is Market Research?

Market Research tells you and whoever is going to back you with money (e.g. your bank) if your business idea is likely to work

***It is a very important part of your business plan!***

Market Research means getting together facts:

- Will a lot of people want to buy the goods or services you want to sell?
- Will people pay the prices you ask?
- Will people still want or need what you are selling a few years from now?
- Are a lot of people selling the same things?
- Are other people selling for less money?
- Are other people giving a better service?

# Market Research

## How to do Market Research 1

- Look at leaflets and reports in your local library
- Use the Internet
- Ask for help to find what you need

Make notes on what you have found out

Take your idea and find out

- What other people have done using an idea like yours
- How well they have done
- If the overall trend is getting better

# Market Research

## How to do Market Research 2

**Find out what people want by:**

- Asking them in person

- Talking to them on the phone
- Sending questions by post

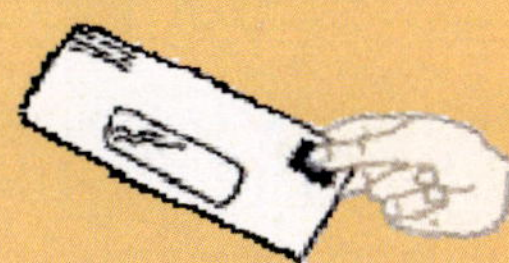

- Using email

***This is called doing a survey***

When you do the survey ...

- People may give you ideas to make your business better.
- You will have a list of names and addresses of people who like your business idea. This can be used as a mailing list

**The results of the survey can be a very important part of your business plan**

# Market Research

## How to do Market Research 3

### Test Marketing

- Try selling the product you make or want to trade to 'real customers'. Make sure your prices are 'real' as well!

- Try offering your services in return for 'real' payment to 'real customers'.

This **Test Marketing** will give you a good idea of how much people will really want to pay for what you are selling.

**Note: If you get benefit payments you will need to let Social Security know what money you get from Test sales.**

**OR**

**You can sell a small amount such as 1 or 2 products or (if selling a service) do 1 or 2 free trials**

**Competitors** are people who have set up a business like the one you have in mind.
You can find out a lot from them about:

- Prices
- What works
- What doesn't work

**Are there a lot of people already trading in your area?**

Look in Yellow Pages to find local **competitors.**

# Market Research

Copy

## More on prices

**Note!**

- too low a price may stop you making a profit
- too high a price may stop people buying from you

**Tip!** Make a note of competitor prices on a chart like this

| Product or Service | Competitor Prices | | | |
|---|---|---|---|---|
| | A | B | C | D |
| | | | | |

# Market Research

## How to do Market Research 4

**Suppliers** are the people who will sell you what you need to run your business.

Go to several **suppliers** and ask for:

- details about what they sell
- price lists

> **Note:** do not rely on just 1 **supplier** in case they have a problem that might make things hard for you

**Letters of Intent** are letters from business people or people who have said they will buy from you.

Ask business people to write a simple letter saying that they plan to buy from you and why (see the sample letter of intent).

> **Note: Ask them to use the headed paper of their business if they have it.**

These letters will show the bank that there are people who want to buy what you are trading.

next page GO

# Market Research

## Example of a letter to a possible supplier using letterhead

***Claire's Cakes***

*113 Treacle Terrace*
*Battenberg*
*Swiss Cottage SW9 99OZ*

*Tel: 01284846209*
*Mobile: 07768263018*
*www.ccaps.co.uk*

10th March 2007

Sweetland Wholesalers
Unit 16
Cherry Orchard Retail Park
Swiss Cottage
SW9 17OX

Dear Sirs

I am looking into where to buy supplies for my cake making business.

Please could you send me any information on your products with prices, discounts and terms of payment.

I look forward to hearing from you.

Yours faithfully

*Claire Baker*

Claire Baker

# Market Research

**Use this example to help you write your own letter**

*Letterhead*
*with your business address etc*

Date

Address of supplier

Dear Sirs

I am looking into where to buy supplies for my *type of trade* business.

Please could you send me any information on your products with prices, discounts and terms of payment.

I look forward to hearing from you.

Yours faithfully

*Your name/signature*

# Market Research

## Letter setting up a meeting with a customer on your own letterhead

***Claire's Cakes***
*113 Treacle Terrace*
*Battenberg*
*Swiss Cottage SW9 99OZ*

*Tel: 01284846209*
*Mobile: 07768263018*
*www.ccaps.co.uk*

10th March 2007

John Coffee
Manager
Bistro Café
Smithson Road
Swiss Cottage
SW4 3OY

Dear Mr Coffee

I am setting up a cake making business. I can offer a wide range of home-made style cakes and pastries that I feel would sell really well in your Bistro Café.

Please could you consider giving some time for a meeting to talk about the possibility of buying cakes from me.

I will telephone you within the next few days in the hope of making an appointment.

Yours sincerely

Claire Baker
Claire Baker

# Market Research

## Testimonial letter

**Organic Foods Supermarket**
**3 – 5 Main Street**
**Sudingham**
**BO4 5 OY**

25th April 2007

To whom it may concern

Re: S. S. Quiggy

Mr Quiggy has worked for us for just over five years as Supervisor for the cleaning of our store; He has been responsible for ordering cleaning materials and allocating work to a small team of operatives.

We have always found him honest, reliable and conscientious and able to work independently and as part of a team.

We wish him every success in this new family venture - Ever Shine Window Cleaning Services.

Yours faithfully

W.D. Oliver
General Manager

# Market Research

## Things to think about!

1. Where can you meet customers who will buy from you?

2. If you are going to have a shop look to see if a lot of people walk past who may want to buy what you are selling.
   Talk to shopkeepers in the area about your ideas.

3. Do you need samples, photos, letters about your character (**testimonial letters**)?

4. How many people do you need to talk to about your idea?

5. Is there a gap that your business can fill?

6. Go to trade shows to find out what other businesses are doing.

# Market Research

Copy

**Think of questions you'd ask to see if someone will buy from you.**

Would you buy this ………………(product or service)?

How much would you pay for this……………(product or service)?

……………………………………………………………………………

……………………………………………………………………………

……………………………………………………………………………

……………………………………………………………………………

……………………………………………………………………………

……………………………………………………………………………

……………………………………………………………………………

……………………………………………………………………………

……………………………………………………………………………

……………………………………………………………………………

# Marketing

## Advertising

**Advertising lets people know about your service or your product. You can advertise by using:**

- **Business cards**
- **Flyers**
- **Local papers**
- **Local radio**
- **Email**
- **Internet**
- **Telephone**

Don't wait until your business has started.

Advertise early so you have customers at the start!

# Finance

**Part 3 of your Business Plan** 

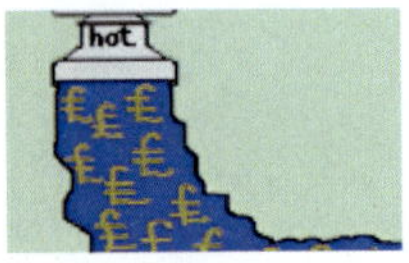

# Cash Flow

**We all use**

## Cash Flow

**We all have money coming in and have to pay money out**

**Pages 74 – 81 show you how to work out your Cash Flow**

**Money out**

Rent
Mortgage
Telephone
Food
Heating
Lighting
Clothes

**out**

**in**

**Money In**
Wages
Benefits

**The trick is to have more money coming in!**

# Cash Flow

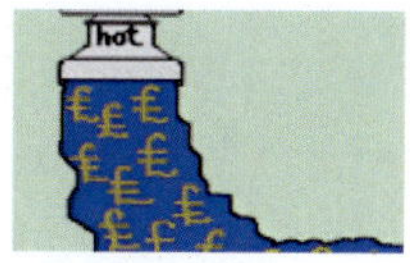

To find out how the cash flows in your home you need to

- Add up [**+**] money coming in (**income**)
- Add up [**+**] money going out (**outgoings**)
- Find out how much money is left by taking away [-] the income from the outgoings

These signs will tell you when to add [+] and when to take away [-]

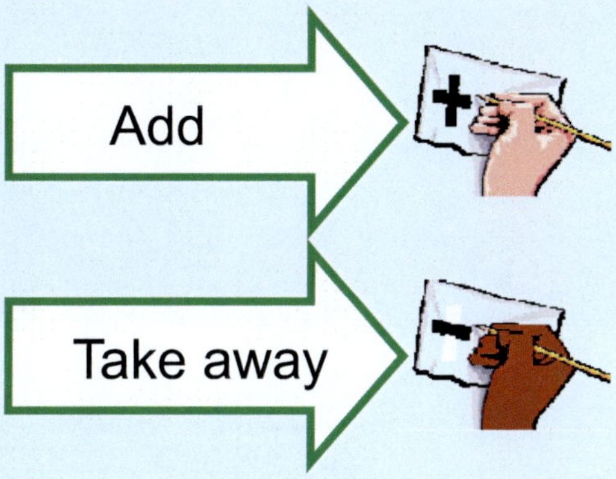


It's OK to use a calculator

***Useful tips for home and business***

Keep all bills and receipts tidy.

Keep them in date order.

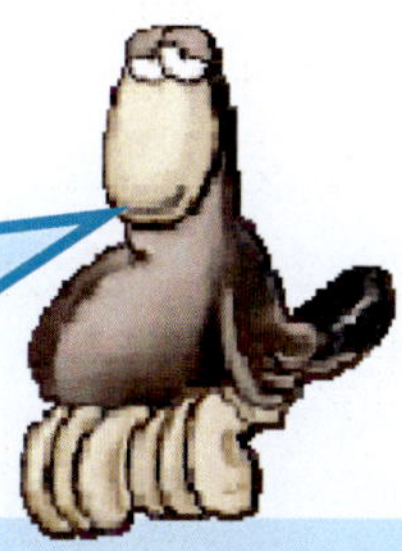

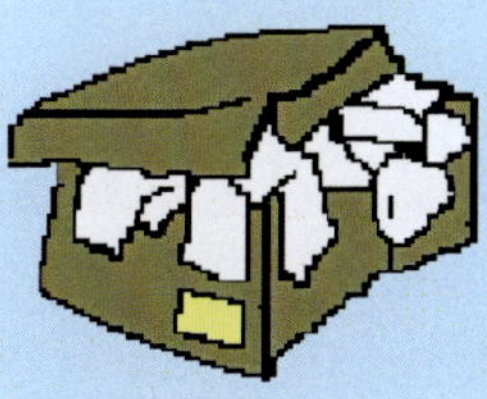

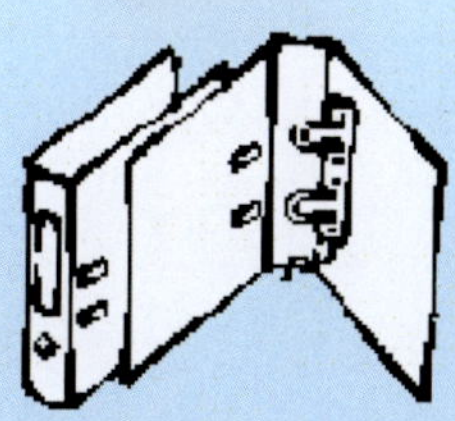

# Cash Flow

Some bills are paid weekly and some are paid monthly.

Some people are paid weekly and some are paid monthly.

Benefits are paid every two weeks

**If you add up all the money coming in and all the money going out for a year it will be for 52 weeks**

Some tips to help you work out Money coming in and Money going out for a month

| S | M | T | W | T | F | S |
|---|---|---|---|---|---|---|
| | | | | | | 1 |
| 2 | 3 | 4 | 5 | 6 | 7 | 8 |
| 9 | 10 | 11 | 12 | 13 | 14 | 15 |
| 16 | 17 | 18 | 19 | 20 | 21 | 22 |
| 23 | 24 | 25 | 26 | 27 | 28 | 29 |
| 30 | 31 | | | | | |

We think of a month as 4 weeks.

- 1 year = 52 weeks
- 12 (months) x 4 (weeks) = 48 weeks
- 52 - 48 = 4 weeks short

**In business we have to work out the money in (income) and money out (outgoings) over 52 weeks**

**To get 52 weeks we make 4 months of the year into 5 week months.**

More on this later!!

# Cash Flow

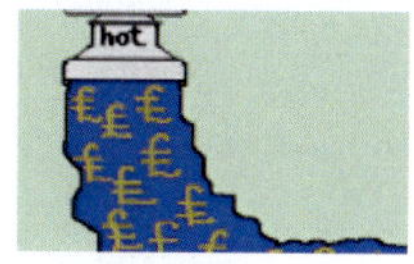


Work out how much money you have coming in for a

- 4 week month ........................................
- 5 week month ........................................

| Item | Amount (£) |
|---|---|
| Rent or mortgage | 240.00 |
| Electric | 25.00 |
| Gas | 22.00 |
| Water Rates | 50.00 |
| Telephone | 40.00 |
| Insurance | 25.00 |
| Television Licence | 11.50 |
| Food and clothes | 140.00 |
| Council Tax | 80.00 |
| Travel | 28.00 |
| Total Income | 850.00 |
| Total Outgoings | 661.50 |
| Balance | 188.50 |

A monthly home cash flow chart could look like this

**The Balance is the money you have left when you take your outgoings from your income**

Think of this chart as a 4 week month record of money in and money out.

When you go on to work out your home cash flow chart work out one for 4 weeks and one for 5 weeks

**Do your sums on next page** GO

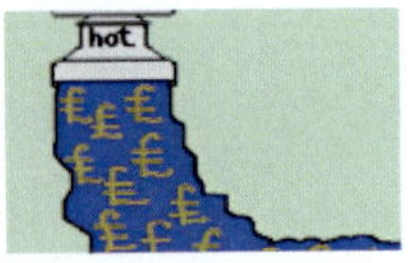

# Cash Flow

- Fill in the chart with the money you pay out each month and add up to get your **outgoings**

- Fill in how much you have coming in (**income**)

| Total Income | - | Total Outgoings | = | Balance |
|---|---|---|---|---|

- Take away **outgoings** from **income** to find the balance

| | 4 week month | 5 week month |
|---|---|---|
| **Item** | **Amount (£)** | **Amount (£)** |
| **Rent or Mortgage** | | |
| **Electric** | | |
| **Gas** | | |
| **Water Rates** | | |
| **Telephone** | | |
| **Insurance** | | |
| **Television Licence/Rental** | | |
| **Food and Clothes** | | |
| **Council Tax** | | |
| **Travel/car** | | |
| **Total Income** | | |
| **Total Outgoings** | | |
| **Balance** | | |

**Use this to help work out your Personal Survival Income**

# Cash Flow

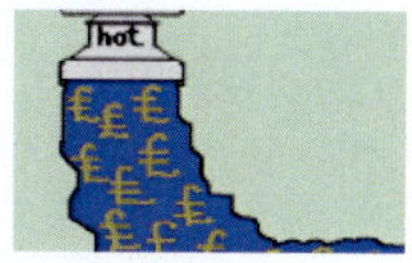

## Personal Survival Income

**Personal Survival Income is money you need to live on. This is how much you have coming in so you can pay your bills (money going out).**

**It will be a lot like your home cash flow but you may want to add in costs for things like holidays.**

It will be what you need for:

- Rent or mortgage
- Business rates or council tax
- Water rates
- Gas, electricity and oil
- Insurance
- Telephone
- Television
- Food and housekeeping
- Clothing
- Car expenses —

You need to know how much you need to live on so you know how much money your business has to make

You may also need money for:

- Family costs
- Credit card or loan repayments

**List and add up your outgoings** GO

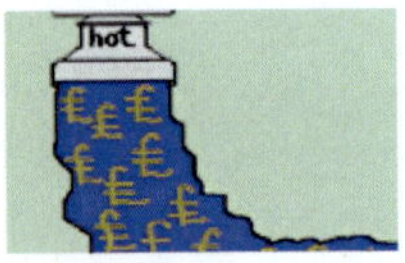




# Cash Flow

## Personal Survival Income

Copy

- This is the money you need to live on
- List what you have to spend money on
- Work out how much you need for a month
- Add some money for the tax you will have to pay
- Use the total outgoings to help you work out how much you will need to pay yourself out of the money your business makes

| Item | Amount (£) |
|---|---|
| | |
| | |
| | |
| | |
| | |
| | |
| | |
| | |
| | |
| | |
| | |
| | |
| | |
| Total Outgoings | |

# Cash Flow

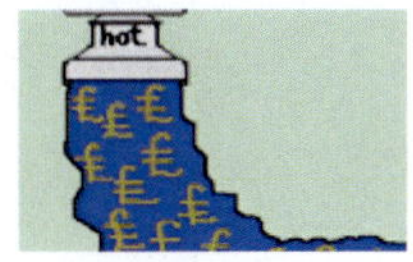

Some of the bills for your business will be like the bills at home. Fill in some amounts on this simple Cash Flow Chart and do the sums

Copy ✓

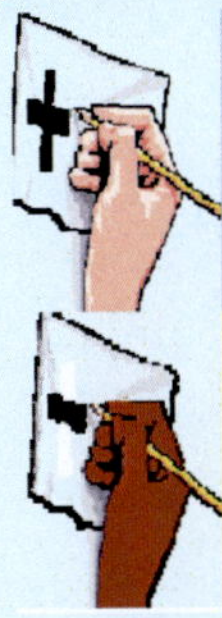

Add money paid out to get total outgoings

Take away outgoings from income to get the balance

| Item (Bills) | Amount Paid (£) |
|---|---|
| Drawings | |
| Business Stock | |
| Travel and Motor | |
| Stationery and Postage | |
| Telephone | |
| Repairs and Maintenance | |
| Rent and Rates | |
| Loan repayments | |
| Heating and Lighting | |
| Total Monthly Income | |
| Total Monthly Outgoings | |
| Total Money Left Over (Balance) | |

**Drawings**: the money you pay yourself out of the business ('wages')

Use your **Personal Survival Income** to help you work this out

**Business Stock**: Items you have paid for to use or sell for your business

**Work out money in and money out from sales**

GO

| Total Income | - | Total Outgoings | = | Balance |
|---|---|---|---|---|

# Financial Assumptions

## Financial Assumptions

This simply means

- **how much money you think you will get from sales (Money in)**

and

- **how much money you think you will have to pay out (Money out)**

## Money in ?

To work out what you think all your sales will add up to in a year you will need to work out

- How many sales you hope to make each week
- How much you will make per week from these sales
- How much money will come in as cash
- How much money will come in as credit
- Total money made from sales

## Money out ?

The cost of what you have to buy in each week (purchases) e.g.

- Cost of goods to sell on
- Cost of goods to make product to sell
- Cost of goods to provide service

There may be times in the year when you sell more (such as December) and other times when you sell less (such as January)



 

# Financial Assumptions

## Claire's Cakes Financial Assumptions

Sales and Purchases - Cash Sales

| Month | No of weeks per month<br>A | No of sales per week<br>B | Selling price per unit<br>C | Total Sales<br>A x B x C | Purchase price per unit<br>D | Total purchases<br>A x B x D |
|---|---|---|---|---|---|---|
| 1 | 4 | 4 | 55.00 | 880.00 | 10.00 | 160.00 |
| 2 | 4 | 4 | 55.00 | 880.00 | 10.00 | 160.00 |
| 3 | 5 | 3 | 45.00 | 675.00 | 6.00 | 90.00 |
| 4 | 4 | 3 | 45.00 | 540.00 | 6.00 | 72.00 |
| 5 | 4 | 2 | 30.00 | 240.00 | 5.00 | 40.00 |
| 6 | 5 | 6 | 30.00 | 900.00 | 5.00 | 150.00 |
| 7 | 4 | 6 | 30.00 | 720.00 | 5.00 | 120.00 |
| 8 | 4 | 2 | 30.00 | 240.00 | 5.00 | 40.00 |
| 9 | 5 | 3 | 30.00 | 450.00 | 5.00 | 75.00 |
| 10 | 4 | 4 | 45.00 | 720.00 | 6.00 | 96.00 |
| 11 | 4 | 6 | 30.00 | 720.00 | 5.00 | 120.00 |
| 12 | 5 | 4 | 30.00 | 600.00 | 5.00 | 100.00 |
| Total | 52 | | | 7565.00 | | 1223.00 |

**Note:** You only have to add up the Total Sales and Total Purchases to get totals to go in a Cash Flow Forecast.

Sales will go in the green part of the forecast (money in)

Purchases will go in the blue part of the Forecast (money out)

Go to next page to find out more

GO

# Financial Assumptions

The form used to work out how many sales you think you will make and how much money you will need to spend to make the sales is called:

**A Financial Assumptions sheet**

In your Business Plan you will do a Financial Assumptions Sheet for **Cash Sales** and **Credit Sales**

### Cash Sales

What you think you will sell using cash.

A cheque payment is cash.

### Credit sales

What you think you will sell to be paid for later on delivery of goods or services

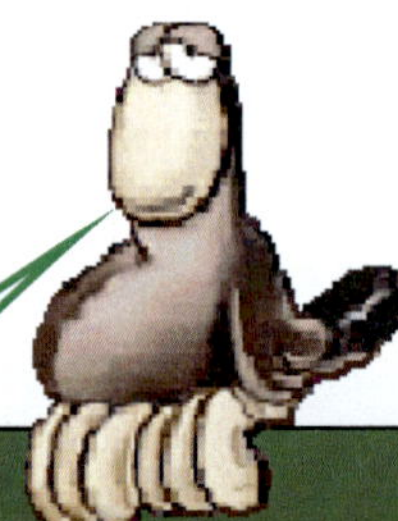

**Your total sales and total purchases will go into your**
**Cash Flow Forecast**

**Go to next page to see what the Financial Assumptions Sheet looks like for Claire's Cakes (Cash Sales)**

# Financial Assumptions

## Cash Sales

To get total purchases multiply (x) the number of weeks in the month (A) by the number of sales (B) by the price you pay (D).

No. of purchases will be the same as no. of sales (B) - you have to buy to be able to sell.

How many sales you sell in a week

**Financial Assumptions**

**Sales and Purchases - Cash Sales**

| Month | No of weeks per month<br>A | No of sales per week<br>B | Selling price per unit<br>C | Total Sales<br>A x B x C | Purchase price per unit<br>D | Total Purchases<br>A x B x D |
|---|---|---|---|---|---|---|
| 1 | 4 | | | | | |
| 2 | 4 | | | | | |
| 3 | 5 | | | | | |

Four months in the year have 5 weeks. 8 months have 4 weeks (More about this in Cash Flow Forecast)

To get total sales multiply (x) the number of weeks in the month (A) by the number of sales (B) then by the price charged (C)

**Note:**
**Work on costs of buying in each week (purchase price) as cash for both Cash Sales and Credit Sales Financial Assumptions Sheets**

# Financial Assumptions

## Credit Sales

Total credit purchases

**weeks x purchases x price**
**A x B x D**

**Total credit sales:**

**weeks x sales x price**
**A x B x C**

## Assumptions

| Sales and Purchases - Credit Sales | | | | | | |
|---|---|---|---|---|---|---|
| Month | No of weeks per month<br>A | No of sales per week<br>B | Selling price per unit<br>C | Total Sales<br>A x B x C | Purchase price per unit<br>D | Total Purchases<br>A x B x D |
| 1 | 4 | | | | | |
| 2 | 4 | | | | | |
| 3 | 5 | | | | | |

**To find out how it all works look at the examples for:**

- **Cash Sales - pages 78-79**
  ***Ever Shine Windows***
- **Credit Sales - pages 82-83**
  ***Claire's Cakes***

# Financial Assumptions

Here we look at how much money a business will charge for cleaning a house with 6 windows - **Selling Price**

**Working out the selling price for a business called Ever Shine Windows (Cash)**

**For one house with 6 windows**

| | |
|---|---|
| • Cost of cleaning materials, cloths etc | £0.50 |
| • Cost of travel | £0.50 |
| • Cost for time (10 minutes) | £3.00 |
| **Total** | **£4.00** |

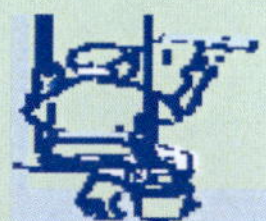

Here we look at how much money we have to spend to clean the windows - **Purchase Price**

**Working out the purchase price for Ever Shine Windows (Cash)**

**For one house with 6 windows**

| | |
|---|---|
| • Cost of cleaning materials, cloths etc | £0.50 |
| • Cost of travel | £0.50 |
| **Total** | **£1.00** |

The selling price and the purchase price for one item is used to work out sales and purchases for each month. The next page will show you how this has been worked out for Ever Shine Windows

next GO

# Financial Assumptions

| Selling price for one house with 6 windows: | Purchase price (cost) for one house with 6 windows: |
|---|---|
| **£4.00** | **£1.00** |

## Ever Shine Windows Financial Assumptions

**Sales and Purchases - Cash Sales**

| Month | No of weeks per month<br>A | No of sales per week<br>B | Selling price per unit<br>C | Total Sales<br>A x B x C | Purchase price per unit<br>D | Total purchases<br>A x B x D |
|---|---|---|---|---|---|---|
| **1** | **4** | 60 | £4.00 | £960.00 | £1.00 | £240.00 |
| **2** | **4** | | | | | |
| **3** | **5** | | | | | |

**Sales and Purchases for Month 1 (May)**

Total Sales = A x B x C = 4 x 60 x £4.00 = £960.00

Total Purchases = A x B x D = 4 x 60 x £1.00 = £240.00

**Note:**

- A window cleaner may not make as many sales in the winter (seasonal fluctuations).
- Month 1 is the first month of trading for this business

**Have a go at filling in the sheet on the next page. Put less sales in for the winter months. Note: Month 1 is May, so month 7 will be November**

GO

# Financial Assumptions

Copy ✓

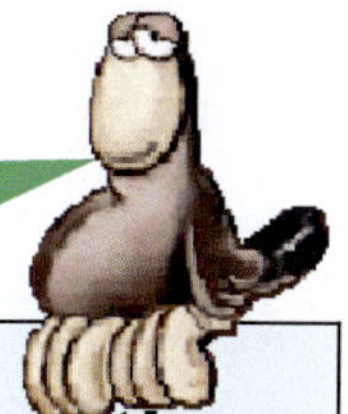

Some figures have been put in to this sheet. Can you fill in the gaps?
**Note:** Don't forget! The number of sales will be less in winter months!

**Month 1 is May**

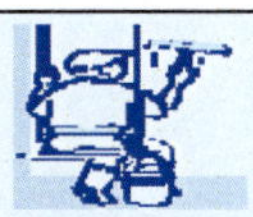

## Ever Shine Windows Financial Assumptions

**Sales and Purchases - Cash Sales**

| Month | No of weeks per month<br>A | No of sales per week<br>B | Selling price per unit<br>C | Total Sales<br>A x B x C | Purchase price per unit<br>D | Total purchases<br>A x B x D |
|---|---|---|---|---|---|---|
| 1 | 4 | 60 | £4.00 | £960.00 | £1.00 | £240.00 |
| 2 | 4 | 70 | £4.00 | | £1.00 | |
| 3 | 5 | 70 | £4.00 | | £1.00 | |
| 4 | 4 | | | | | |
| 5 | 4 | | | | | |
| 6 | 5 | | | | | |
| 7 | 4 | 30 | £4.00 | | £1.00 | |
| 8 | 4 | | | | | |
| 9 | 5 | | | | | |
| 10 | 4 | | | | | |
| 11 | 4 | | | | | |
| 12 | 5 | | | | | |
| Total | 52 | | | | | |

# Financial Assumptions

Copy ✓

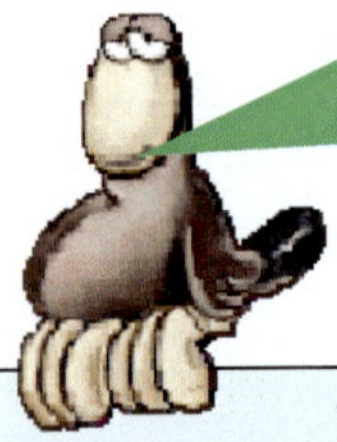

Now have a go at filling in a sheet for your own business.
Make month 1 a month when you would like to start your business

**Month 1 is**

## My Business Financial Assumptions

### Sales and Purchases - Cash Sales

| Month | No of weeks per month<br>A | No of sales per week<br>B | Selling price per unit<br>C | Total Sales<br>A x B x C | Purchase price per unit<br>D | Total purchases<br>A x B x D |
|---|---|---|---|---|---|---|
| 1 | 4 | | | | | |
| 2 | 4 | | | | | |
| 3 | 5 | | | | | |
| 4 | 4 | | | | | |
| 5 | 4 | | | | | |
| 6 | 5 | | | | | |
| 7 | 4 | | | | | |
| 8 | 4 | | | | | |
| 9 | 5 | | | | | |
| 10 | 4 | | | | | |
| 11 | 4 | | | | | |
| 12 | 5 | | | | | |
| Total | 52 | | | | | |

# Financial Assumptions

Claire has a weekly order from a local café/shop for pies and cakes. She sells

- large cream cakes at £5.00 each
- large fruit pies at 2 for £5.00
- small cakes at 24 for £5.00

The order is the same for most of the year but is bigger in July, August and in December (mince pies!)

## Working out the selling price for Claire's Cakes (Credit)

### Cost based on one large cream cake (gateau)

| | |
|---|---|
| • Cost of flour, sugar, butter etc | £1.75 |
| • Gas (oven) | £0.40 |
| • Hot water/washing up liquid | £0.10 |
| • Cost of travel to deliver | £0.25 |
| • Cost for time (labour charge) | £3.00 |
| **Total** | **£5.00** |

## Working out the purchase price for Claire's Cakes (Credit)

### To supply range of pies and small cakes to local café

| | |
|---|---|
| • Cost of ingredients and cooking | £1.75 |
| • Cost of travel to deliver | £0.25 |
| **Total** | **£2.00** |

# Financial Assumptions

## Claire's Cakes Financial Assumptions

| Sales and Purchases - Credit Sales | | | | | | |
|---|---|---|---|---|---|---|
| Month | No of weeks per month<br>A | No of sales per week<br>B | Selling price per unit<br>C | Total Sales<br>A x B x C | Purchase price per unit<br>D | Total purchases<br>A x B x D |
| 1 | 4 | 54 | £5.00 | £1080 | £2.00 | £432 |
| 2 | 4 | 60 | £5.00 | £1200 | £2.00 | £480 |
| 3 | 5 | 60 | £5.00 | £1500 | £2.00 | £600 |

**The selling price is £5.00.**

**Month 1 is June**

**The number of sales per week in month 1 will be 54**

**The selling price per week will be £5.00**

**Month 1 Total Sales: 4 x 54 x £5.00 = £1080.00**

**Month 3 Total Sales: 5 x 60 x £5.00 = £1500.00**

**The purchase price is £2.00**

**Month 1 Total Purchases: 4 x 54 x £2.00 = £432**

**Month 2 Total Purchases: 5 x 60 x £2.00 = £600**

Fill in the gaps for Claire's Cakes on next page

# Financial Assumptions

Copy

Fill in this Credit Sales using the info on Claire's Cakes

Month 1 is June

## Claire's Cakes Financial Assumptions

| Sales and Purchases - Credit Sales | | | | | | |
|---|---|---|---|---|---|---|
| Month | No of weeks per month<br>A | No of sales per week<br>B | Selling price per unit<br>C | Total Sales<br>A x B x C | Purchase price per unit<br>D | Total purchases<br>A x B x D |
| 1 | 4 | 54 | £5.00 | | £2.00 | |
| 2 | 4 | | | | | |
| 3 | 5 | 60 | £5.00 | | £2.00 | |
| 4 | 4 | | | | | |
| 5 | 4 | | | | | |
| 6 | 5 | | | | | |
| 7 | 4 | 70 | £5.00 | | £2.00 | |
| 8 | 4 | | | | | |
| 9 | 5 | | | | | |
| 10 | 4 | | | | | |
| 11 | 4 | | | | | |
| 12 | 5 | | | | | |
| Total | 52 | | | | | |

# Financial Assumptions

Copy ✓

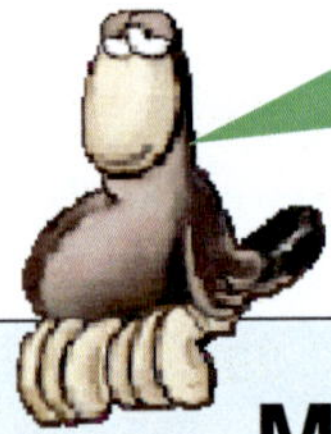

**Now have a go at filling in a Credit Sales sheet for your business**

**Month 1 is**

## My Business Financial Assumptions

### Sales and Purchases - Credit Sales

| Month | No of weeks per month<br>A | No of sales per week<br>B | Selling price per unit<br>C | Total Sales<br>A x B x C | Purchase price per unit<br>D | Total purchases<br>A x B x D |
|---|---|---|---|---|---|---|
| 1 | 4 | | | | | |
| 2 | 4 | | | | | |
| 3 | 5 | | | | | |
| 4 | 4 | | | | | |
| 5 | 4 | | | | | |
| 6 | 5 | | | | | |
| 7 | 4 | | | | | |
| 8 | 4 | | | | | |
| 9 | 5 | | | | | |
| 10 | 4 | | | | | |
| 11 | 4 | | | | | |
| 12 | 5 | | | | | |
| Total | 52 | | | | | |

# Financial Assumptions

To sum up ...

Your Financial Assumptions sheets show you:

- how much money you hope to make
- how much money you think you will have to spend

Note:

To get the total Purchase price for your Cash Flow Forecast you will have to add your Total Purchases for Cash Sales to your Total Purchases for Credit Sales

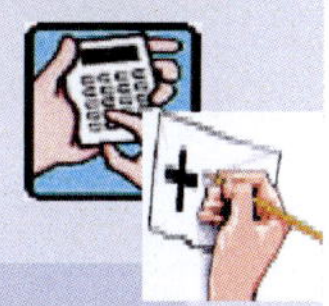

**Claire's Cakes**

| Month | Cash Sales: Total purchases A x B x D | Credit Sales: Total purchases A x B x D |
|---|---|---|
| 1 | **£160.00** | **£432** |
| 2 | £160.00 | £480 |
| 3 | £90.00 | £600 |

**For month 1 Claire's total purchases will be**

**£160** + **£432** = £592

Now do months 2 and 3:

£160 + £480 = £

£90 + £600 = £

**Now add up the total purchases for your business**

# Financial Assumptions

Copy ✓

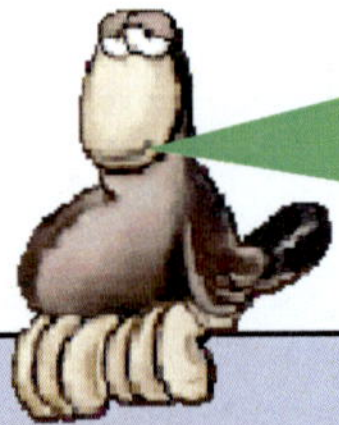

- Copy the numbers from your Business Financial Assumptions Sheet and add them up
- Your totals will go into your Cash Flow Forecast on the line called Business Stock

| Total Purchases for My Business (Business Stock) | | | | | |
|---|---|---|---|---|---|
| | **Cash Sales** | | **Credit Sales** | | |
| **Month** | Total Purchases | | Total Purchases | | Total Purchases |
| **1** | | + | | = | |
| **2** | | + | | = | |
| **3** | | + | | = | |
| **4** | | + | | = | |
| **5** | | + | | = | |
| **6** | | + | | = | |
| **7** | | + | | = | |
| **8** | | + | | = | |
| **9** | | + | | = | |
| **10** | | + | | = | |
| **11** | | + | | = | |
| **12** | | + | | = | |
| **Total** | | + | | = | |

**Find out a bit about Start Up and then go on to do your Cash Flow Forecast** GO

# Start Up

**Start Up** is the money you need to get your business going. Here is a list of some things you may need money for:

- Money to live on (Personal Survival Budget)
- Money to pay for rent of room or office etc
- Money to buy goods to sell, to buy what you need for your service or to make your product
- Money to run a car or van

- You may have your own money

  ( **Money Introduced** on a Cash Flow Forecast)

- You may be able to borrow money from family or friends

  (**Loan** on a Cash Flow Forecast)

- Some small grants are available

  (**Grant** on a Cash Flow Forecast)

- You can take out a loan

  (**Loan** on a Cash Flow Forecast)

# Cash Flow Forecast

See how much money comes in
See how much money goes out
Best to note the date
So you don't run out!

A **Cash Flow Forecast** tells you how **much** money is **due in** and **due out** and **when**

# Cash Flow Forecast

So far we have looked at:

- Cash Flow 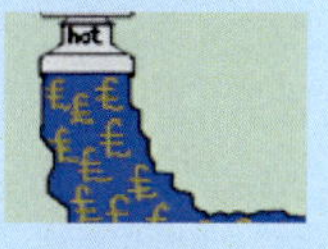
- Personal Survival Budget 
- Financial Assumptions 

- Start Up 

**Now we put it all together in a Cash Flow Forecast**

A Forecast is about looking ahead.

To do a Cash Flow Forecast you look ahead for the next 12 months and work out for each month::

- How much **money** you will have coming **in**
- How much **money** you will have to pay **out** (Drawings + **all** business costs)

The blank Forecast on the next page has been coloured to show

**money in** and **money out**

Copy

## Cash Flow Forecast: This is what a blank forecast looks like.

Find out more step by step

| Number of weeks | | 4 | 4 | 5 | 4 | 4 | 5 | 4 | 4 | 5 | 4 | 4 | 5 | |
|---|---|---|---|---|---|---|---|---|---|---|---|---|---|---|
| **Month** | **Start Up** | 1 | 2 | 3 | 4 | 5 | 6 | 7 | 8 | 9 | 10 | 11 | 12 | Total |
| Cash Sales | | | | | | | | | | | | | | |
| Credit Sales | | | | | | | | | | | | | | |
| Bank Loan | | | | | | | | | | | | | | |
| Loan (family/friends) | | | | | | | | | | | | | | |
| Grant | | | | | | | | | | | | | | |
| Cash Introduced | | | | | | | | | | | | | | |
| Total Receipts (A) | | | | | | | | | | | | | | |
| | | | | | | | | | | | | | | |
| Business Stock | | | | | | | | | | | | | | |
| Drawings | | | | | | | | | | | | | | |
| Telephone | | | | | | | | | | | | | | |
| Stationery and Postage | | | | | | | | | | | | | | |
| Travel and Motor | | | | | | | | | | | | | | |
| Repairs and Maintenance | | | | | | | | | | | | | | |
| Heating and Lighting | | | | | | | | | | | | | | |
| Rent and Rates | | | | | | | | | | | | | | |
| Insurance | | | | | | | | | | | | | | |
| | | | | | | | | | | | | | | |
| Loan Repayments | | | | | | | | | | | | | | |
| Total Repayments (B) | | | | | | | | | | | | | | |
| A-B | | | | | | | | | | | | | | |
| Opening Balance | | | | | | | | | | | | | | |
| Closing Balance | | | | | | | | | | | | | | |

# Cash Flow Forecast

## What words mean?

| | |
|---|---|
| **Cash Sales** | All money in |
| **Credit Sales** | Sales made to be paid for later on delivery of goods or services |
| **Bank Loan** | Money lent by bank (have to repay with Interest) |
| **Loan from family or friend** | Money lent that you may have to pay back but may not pay so much interest, if any |
| **Grant** | Money given (no repayment needed) |
| **Cash Introduced** | Money put in by you (no repayment needed) |
| **Total Receipts (A)** | Total money in |

| | |
|---|---|
| **Business Stock** | 1. Stock sold in a given month<br>2. Stock not sold |
| **Drawings** | What you pay yourself |
| **Telephone** | Cost of phone calls, line rental |
| **Stationery and Postage** | Letters, stamps, business cards, flyers etc |
| **Travel and Motor** | Travel costs (Train/bus etc). Vehicle costs: fuel, servicing, repairs, tax, MOT, insurance etc |
| **Repairs and Maintenance** | 1.Start up costs (eg shop fittings, painting)<br>2. Work on building, tools |
| **Heating and Lighting** | Cost of heating and lighting |
| **Business Insurance** | Building, tools, accident etc |
| **Rent and Rates** | Rent, business rates |
| **Loan Repayments** | Money paid back |
| **Total Payments (B)** | Total money out |
| **(A - B)** | Total receipts – total payments |
| **Opening Balance** | Money you start with at beginning of month |
| **Closing Balance** | Money you are left with at end of month (all money in take away all money out) |

# Cash Flow Forecast

## Step 1: Working out weeks in the month

| | | | | | | | | | | | | | | |
|---|---|---|---|---|---|---|---|---|---|---|---|---|---|---|
| Number of weeks | | 4 | 4 | 5 | 4 | 4 | 5 | 4 | 4 | 5 | 4 | 4 | 5 | |
| **Month** | **Start Up** | 1 | 2 | 3 | 4 | 5 | 6 | 7 | 8 | 9 | 10 | 11 | 12 | Total |

This is the number of weeks in the month

| | | | | | |
|---|---|---|---|---|---|
| **Number of Weeks** | | **4** | **4** | **5** | |
| **Month** | **Start up** | **1** | **2** | **3** | **Total** |

**Total:** total of money

**Start Up:** all money in and money out that you paid when starting your business

Month 1 of Start Up is the month you start in business

We think of a month as 4 weeks.

- 1 year = 52 weeks
- 12 (months) x 4 (weeks) = 48 weeks
- 52 - 48 = 4 weeks short
- To get 52 weeks on a Cash Flow
- Forecast we make 4 months of the year into 5 week months to give us:

| | | | | | | | | | | | | |
|---|---|---|---|---|---|---|---|---|---|---|---|---|
| Number of Weeks | 4 | 4 | 5 | 4 | 4 | 5 | 4 | 4 | 5 | 4 | 4 | 5 |

| M | T | W | T | F | S |
|---|---|---|---|---|---|
| | | | | | 1 |
| | 4 | 5 | 6 | 7 | 8 |
| | 11 | 12 | 13 | 14 | 15 |
| | 18 | 19 | 20 | 21 | 22 |
| 24 | 25 | 26 | 27 | 28 | 29 |
| 31 | | | | | |

# Cash Flow Forecast

## Step 2: Adding money coming in

All money coming in

| | |
|---|---|
| Cash Sales | |
| Credit Sales | |
| Bank Loan | 8000.00 |
| Loan from family or friends | |
| Grant | |
| Cash Introduced | 2000.00 |
| Total Receipts (A) | |

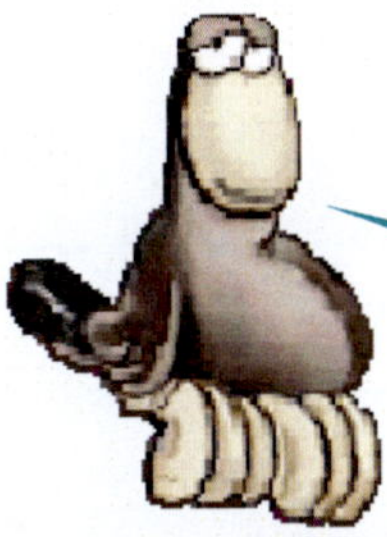

**To get Total Receipts (A) under Start Up add (+) down ↓**

## Step 3: Adding money going out

| | |
|---|---|
| Business Stock | 190.00 |
| Drawings | |
| Telephone | 110.00 |
| Stationery and Postage | 125.00 |
| Travel and Motor | |
| Repairs and Maintenance | |
| Heating and Lighting | |
| Rent and Rates | |
| Loan Repayments | |
| Total Payments (B) | |

All money paid out

**To get Total Payments (B) under Start Up add (+) down ↓**

# Cash Flow Forecast

The Cash Flow Chart so far

| Number of Weeks | | 4 | 4 | 5 | |
|---|---|---|---|---|---|
| Month | Start Up | 1 | 2 | 3 | Total |
| Cash Sales | | | | | |
| Credit Sales | | | | | |
| Loan (Bank) | 8000.00 | | | | |
| Cash Introduced | 2000.00 | | | | |
| Total Receipts (A) | 10000.00 | | | | |
| | | | | | |
| Business Stock | 190.00 | | | | |
| Drawings | | | | | |
| Telephone | 110.00 | | | | |
| Stationery and Postage | 125.00 | | | | |
| Travel and Motor | | | | | |
| Repairs and Maintenance | | | | | |
| Heating and Lighting | | | | | |
| Rent and Rates | | | | | |
| Loan Repayments | | | | | |
| Total Payments (B) | 425.00 | | | | |

All money coming in

All money paid out

next page GO

Money Matters

# Cash Flow Forecast

## Step 4: A (Receipts) - B (Payments)

| Number of Weeks | | 4 | 4 | 5 | |
|---|---|---|---|---|---|
| Month | Start Up | 1 | 2 | 3 | Total |
| Cash Sales | | | | | |
| Credit Sales | | | | | |
| Bank Loan | 8000.00 | | | | |
| Loan (family/friends) | | | | | |
| Grant | | | | | |
| Cash Introduced | 2000.00 | | | | |
| Total Receipts (A) | 10000.00 | | | | |
| | | | | | |
| Business Stock | 190.00 | | | | |
| Drawings | | | | | |
| Telephone | 110.00 | | | | |
| Stationery and Postage | 125.00 | | | | |
| Travel and Motor | | | | | |
| Repairs and Maintenance | | | | | |
| Heating/Lighting | | | | | |
| Rent and Rates | | | | | |
| Loan Repayments | | | | | |
| Total Payments (B) | 425.00 | | | | |
| A - B | 9575.00 | | | | |

No money for sales under Start up as not yet trading

**Cash Introduced:** your own money

**To get A - B the sum is:**

**Total Receipts - Total Payments**

$$
\begin{array}{r}
10000.00 \\
- \quad \underline{425.00} \\
9575.00
\end{array}
$$

| | |
|---|---|
| Total Receipts (A) | 10000.00 |
| Total Payments (B) | 425.00 |
| A - B | 9575.00 |

next page

# Cash Flow Forecast

## Step 5: Opening Balance

| Number of Weeks | | 4 | 4 | 5 | |
|---|---|---|---|---|---|
| Month | Start Up | 1 | 2 | 3 | Total |
| Cash Sales | | | | | |
| Credit Sales | | | | | |
| Bank Loan | 8000.00 | | | | |
| Loan (family or friends) | | | | | |
| Grant | | | | | |
| Cash Introduced | 2000.00 | | | | |
| Total Receipts (A) | 10000.00 | | | | |
| | | | | | |
| Business Stock | | | | | |
| Drawings | | | | | |
| Telephone | | | | | |
| Stationery and Post-age | | | | | |
| Travel and Motor | | | | | |
| Repairs/Maintenance | | | | | |
| Heating and Lighting | | | | | |
| Rent and Rates | | | | | |
| Loan Repayments | | | | | |
| Total Payments (B) | 425.00 | | | | |
| A - B | 9575.00 | | | | |
| Opening Balance | 000.00 | | | | |

| | |
|---|---|
| Opening Balance | 000.00 |

The **Opening Balance under start up** is £000.00: nothing has been put in or taken out

next page

# Cash Flow Forecast

## Step 6: Closing Balance

| Number of Weeks | | 4 | 4 | 5 | |
|---|---|---|---|---|---|
| Month | Start Up | 1 | 2 | 3 | Total |
| Cash Sales | | | | | |
| Credit Sales | | | | | |
| Bank Loan | | | | | |
| Loan (family/ friends) | | | | | |
| Grant | | | | | |
| Cash Introduced | | | | | |
| Total Receipts (A) | [illegible] | | | | |
| | | | | | |
| Business Stock | 190.00 | | | | |
| Drawings | | | | | |
| Telephone | 110.00 | | | | |
| Stationery and Postage | 125.00 | | | | |
| Travel and Motor | | | | | |
| Repairs and Maintenance | | | | | |
| Heating and Light-ing | | | | | |
| Rent and Rates | | | | | |
| Loan Repayments | | | | | |
| Total Payments (B) | | | | | |
| A - B | | | | | |
| Opening Balance | 000.00 | 9575.00 | | | |
| Closing Balance | 9575.00 | | | | |

| Closing Balance | 9575.00 |
|---|---|

The **Closing Balance** is:

**all money in minus ( - ) all money out**

**The closing balance is what you get at the end of a month.**

This has to be carried forward. All this means is that it becomes the opening balance for the next month.

next page

# Cash Flow Forecast

The totals for **Sales** (Money in) worked out in **Financial Assumptions** go into the boxes for **Cash Sales** and **Credit Sales**

The total for **Purchases** (Money out) from your **Financial Assumptions** goes under **Business Stock**

When all the figures have been put into the chart it is time to start adding them up! You have to add down and across

| **Number of Weeks** | | 4 | 4 | | |
|---|---|---|---|---|---|
| **Month** | **Start Up** | 1 | 2 | 3 | |
| Cash Sales | 5000.00 | 250.00 | 200.00 | 225.00 | |
| Credit Sales | | | | 4853.50 | |
| Bank Loan | 3000.00 | | | | |
| Loan (family/friends) | 2000.00 | | | | |
| Grant | | | | | |
| Cash Introduced | | | | | |
| **Total Receipts (A)** | | | | | |
| Business Stock | | 201.48 | 201.48 | 201.48 | |
| Drawings | | 800.00 | 800.00 | 800.00 | |
| Telephone | 125.00 | 40.00 | 40.00 | 40.00 | |
| Stationary & Post-age | 110.00 | 20.00 | 22.00 | 21.00 | |
| Travel & Motor | | 45.00 | 45.00 | 45.00 | |
| Repair & Mainte-nance | | | | | |
| Heating & Lighting | | 45.00 | 45.00 | 45.00 | |
| Rent & Rates | | 60.00 | 60.00 | 60.00 | |
| Loan repayments | | | | 50.00 | |
| **Total Payments (B)** | | | | | |
| **A - B** | | | | | |
| **Opening Balance** | | | | | |
| **Closing Balance** | | | | | |

**Step: 7 Add Down**

**+ Down**

**Step: 8 Add Across**

**+ Across**

**Work out some totals on next page** GO

# Cash Flow Forecast

**Step: 7 Add Down** 7 — **+ Down**

**Step: 8 Add** **+ Across** 8

| Number of Wee |  | 4 | 4 |  | Totals |
|---|---|---|---|---|---|
| **Month** | **Start Up** | **1** | **2** | **3** |  |
| Cash Sales | 5000.00 | 250.00 | 200.00 | 225.00 |  |
| Credit Sales |  |  |  | 4853.50 |  |
| Bank Loan | 3000.00 |  |  |  |  |
| Loan (family/friends) | 2000.00 |  |  |  |  |
| Grant |  |  |  |  |  |
| Cash Introduced |  |  |  |  |  |
| **Total Receipts (A)** |  |  |  |  |  |

| | | | | | |
|---|---|---|---|---|---|
| Business Stock |  | 201.48 | 201.48 | 201.48 |  |
| Drawings |  | 800.00 | 800.00 | 800.00 |  |
| Telephone | 125.00 | 40.00 | 40.00 | 40.00 |  |
| Stationary & Postage | 110.00 | 20.00 | 22.00 | 21.00 |  |
| Travel & Motor |  | 45.00 | 45.00 | 45.00 |  |
| Repair & Maintenance |  |  |  |  |  |
| Heating & Lighting |  | 45.00 | 45.00 | 45.00 |  |
| Rent & Rates |  | 60.00 | 60.00 | 60.00 |  |
| Loan repayments |  |  |  | 50.00 |  |
| **Total Payments (B)** |  |  |  |  |  |
| **A - B** |  |  |  |  |  |
| **Opening Balance** |  |  |  |  |  |
| **Closing Balance** |  |  |  |  |  |

# Cash Flow Forecast

## Tips

- Use your Financial Assumption Sheets to fill in:

Cash Sales 

Credit Sales 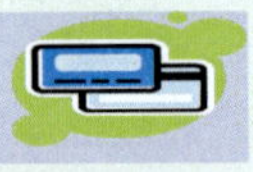

Business Stock

- How to work out **Heating and Lighting** if you work from home:

Say your home has 5 rooms and you use 1 room as your office. Take your bills for gas etc and work out how much the total will be if shared out into 5 equal parts. One part (one fifth) can be put into your Cash Flow Forecast

- How to work out **Rent and Rates** if you work from home:

Do the same as for Heating and lighting; take your rent (or mortgage) and your Council Tax and share the total into 5 equal parts. One part (one fifth) can go into your Forecast

Now for your Cash Flow Forecast!

Have a go at filling this in

# Cash Flow Forecast

Copy

| Number of weeks | | 4 | 4 | 5 | 4 | 4 | 5 | 4 | 4 | 5 | 4 | 4 | 5 | |
|---|---|---|---|---|---|---|---|---|---|---|---|---|---|---|
| **Month** | **Start Up** | 1 | 2 | 3 | 4 | 5 | 6 | 7 | 8 | 9 | 10 | 11 | 12 | Total |
| Cash Sales | | | | | | | | | | | | | | |
| Credit Sales | | | | | | | | | | | | | | |
| Bank Loan | | | | | | | | | | | | | | |
| Loan (family/friends) | | | | | | | | | | | | | | |
| Grant | | | | | | | | | | | | | | |
| Cash Introduced | | | | | | | | | | | | | | |
| Total Receipts (A) | | | | | | | | | | | | | | |
| | | | | | | | | | | | | | | |
| Business Stock | | | | | | | | | | | | | | |
| Drawings | | | | | | | | | | | | | | |
| Telephone | | | | | | | | | | | | | | |
| Stationery and Postage | | | | | | | | | | | | | | |
| Travel and Motor | | | | | | | | | | | | | | |
| Repairs and Maintenance | | | | | | | | | | | | | | |
| Heating and Lighting | | | | | | | | | | | | | | |
| Rent and Rates | | | | | | | | | | | | | | |
| Insurance | | | | | | | | | | | | | | |
| | | | | | | | | | | | | | | |
| Loan Repayments | | | | | | | | | | | | | | |
| Total Repayments (B) | | | | | | | | | | | | | | |
| A-B | | | | | | | | | | | | | | |
| Opening Balance | | | | | | | | | | | | | | |
| Closing Balance | | | | | | | | | | | | | | |

# Break Even

If you have a loan you will have to put a **break even** into your business plan

£ = £

- A **break even** tells you when you will start to make a profit
- It will show you if your business is likely to work

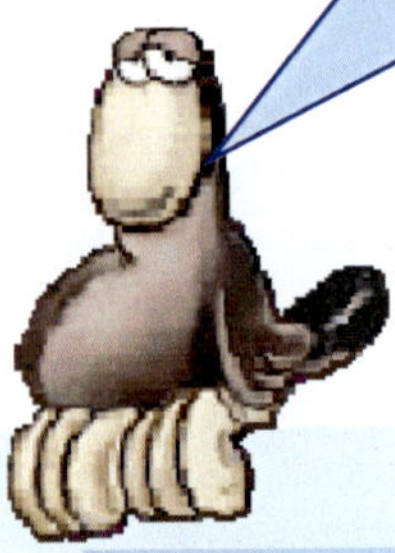

**To find out what the break even is for your business work out how much you need to sell to cover your business costs**

**What you make after this point will be profit**

As part of your fixed costs (overheads) remember to add in any payments you make quarterly or per year (e.g. tax)

Money Matters

# Break Even

**Working it out!**

A product sells for £20

The product costs the business £14

£20 - £14 = £6

**This means that the business has £6 to put towards the cost of overheads. If the overheads for the year come to £15000 you will have to sell 2500 products (2500 x 6 = 15000) to break even**

**Step 1**

It costs Claire £2 to make a cake:

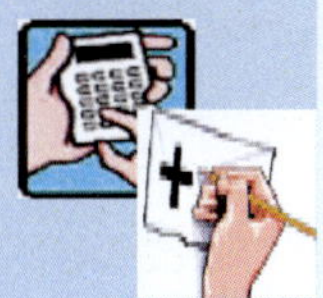

| | |
|---|---|
| Flour, sugar, butter etc | £1.40 |
| Gas (oven) | £0.25 |
| Washing up liquid/hot water | £0.10 |
| Delivery | £0.25 |
| **Total** | **£2.00** |

**Some overheads are added into the £2.00** (oven, hot water) **but not overheads like rent, telephone, drawings.**

She sells the cake for £5 **£5 - £2 = £3**

- **Claire has £3 to put to the cost of overheads**

Next step

# Break Even

**Step 2**

Claire has overheads of £15000

To find out how many cakes she will have to sell to cover this cost and break even she does this sum:

**15000 ÷ 3 = 5000**

**(We can also write it like this:** $\frac{15000}{3} = 5000$**)**

If we put Step 1 and Step 2 together we make this sum:

$$\frac{\text{Overheads (£15000)}}{\text{Unit price (£5) – unit purchase cost (£2)}}$$

For Claire the sum in numbers is: $\frac{£15000}{£5 - £2} = 5000$

To make your sum use your Cash Flow Forecast to get:

- Overheads (total payments)
- Unit price
- Unit purchase cost



 

# Info Pages

## Useful stuff to check out

- Profit and Loss Account

- Balance Sheet
- A bit on Tax, N.I. and VAT
- Samples of cheques, paying-in slips, invoices, receipts, forms
- Tips for Business Cards
- Useful Websites
- Links to more Help and Support

# Profit and Loss Account

**What you make is a profit**
**What you don't want is a loss**
**'Cos if you have that**
**You won't make a lot!**

## Why you need to work out your profit

- To find out how much tax you will have to pay
- To tell you how much the business is worth if you want to sell it
- To tell you and others how much money you have made

**You do not have to put a profit and loss account in your Business Plan**

Note!

Loss doesn't just mean money lost; it is money that you have paid out on your business.

See next page for what words mean on a Profit and Loss Account

# Profit and Loss Account

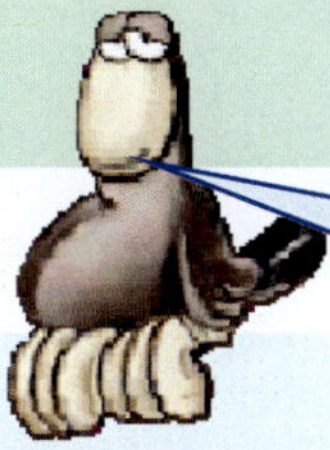

## Words you may find in a Profit and Loss Account

- **Turnover =** Money you make from selling goods or supplying a service. This is the same as net income.
- **Cost Of Goods Sold =** Money you have paid out for your supplies.
- **Other Costs and Trading Costs =** Money you pay out to keep the business running (but not stock).
- **Gross Profit** = turnover less the cost of goods sold
- **Net Profit =** money you have left
- **Other Income =** grants for example
- **Drawings =** money you take out of the business to live on (wage)
- **Retained Profit =** Net profit less drawings (i.e. money that is left in the business)
- **Tax =** money your business has to pay the Government (Tax is paid on the Net Profit)
- **Depreciation =** loss of value e.g. on car because of use
- **Bad debts =** money you will not get for goods sold because of non payment (on credit sales)

# Balance Sheet

**Put your money in**
**Take away the money out**
**This gives you the balance**
**Of your business account**

A **Balance Sheet** tells you what the business owns and what it owes at a set point in time.

- **What a Company owns = Assets**
- **What a Company owes money for = Liabilities**

See next page for what other words mean on a Balance Sheet

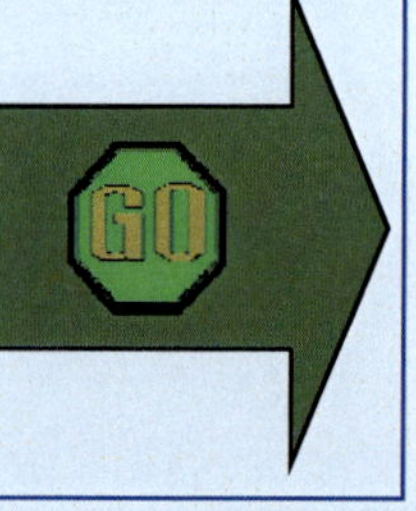


A Balance Sheet is used

- To show the value of your business
- To show how much a business is worth at a set time e.g. at the end of the month.

# Balance Sheet

**Just to let you know what words mean on a Balance Sheet**

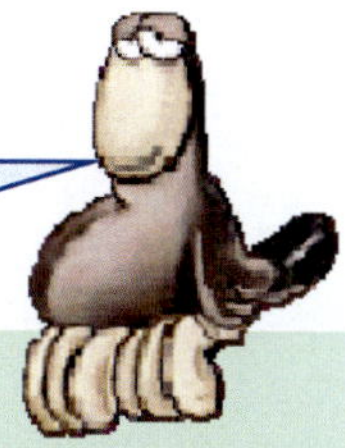

**Fixed Assets**
Items your business owns: computer, car, vans, kitchen equipment, tools,

**Current Assets**
Stock, money owed to company, money in bank account.

**Current liabilities**
Loans, money owed.

**Net Assets**
Money after loan taken away.

**Share Capital =** money owed to people who have given you money to start your business. **Not bank loans**

**Retained Profit**
Money that is put back into the company

**Capital**
All money used by business

# A bit about Tax and NI contributions

## Tax

- You will still have to pay tax when you have your own business.
- Income tax can be called a personal liability—it is what you have to pay on what you earn
- If you are a sole trader or a partnership you will pay income tax out of your drawings. Make sure you add in the money you will need to do this.
- You will have to pay tax on the profit your business makes. Tax is paid on the Net Profit
- You do not have to pay tax for example on a grant from the Prince's Trust

## National Insurance (NI)

- You may not have to pay NI. This depends on how much money your business makes. You will need to get a small earnings **Certificate of Exception** from HMRC

**Call your local HM Revenue and Customs office to find out more about Tax and National Insurance**

# What is VAT?

**Value Added Tax (VAT)** is :

- a direct tax (on what you earn) and
- an indirect tax (on what the customer spends at your business)

**Standard rate is 17.5 %**

**Registering for VAT**

You do not **have** to register until turnover of business is more than £64,000 in a year (2007 figure) but if your cash flow forecast shows your turnover to be near this it is best to register for VAT from day 1 of your business.

Tel Advice Line: 0845 010 9000
Customs website: www.hmce.gsi.gov.uk

Copy ✓

# Sample blank cheque - filled in

Date 13th January 2006

Pay P M Smithersons

Old Balance 1250.00

£ 250.00

New Balance 1000.00

000001

**Bank of Barryville**

Bank of Barryville, High Street, Greater Barryville, BB1 1BB

**22-00-78**

**00987654**

Date 13th January 2006

**Pay** Phillip Matrin Smitherson

Two Hundred and Fifty Pounds Only

Account Payee

£250.00

C Baker

**C Baker**

| Cheque No | Sort Code | Account Number |
| --- | --- | --- |
| 000001 | 22-00-78 | 00987654 |

Copy

# Sample blank cheque

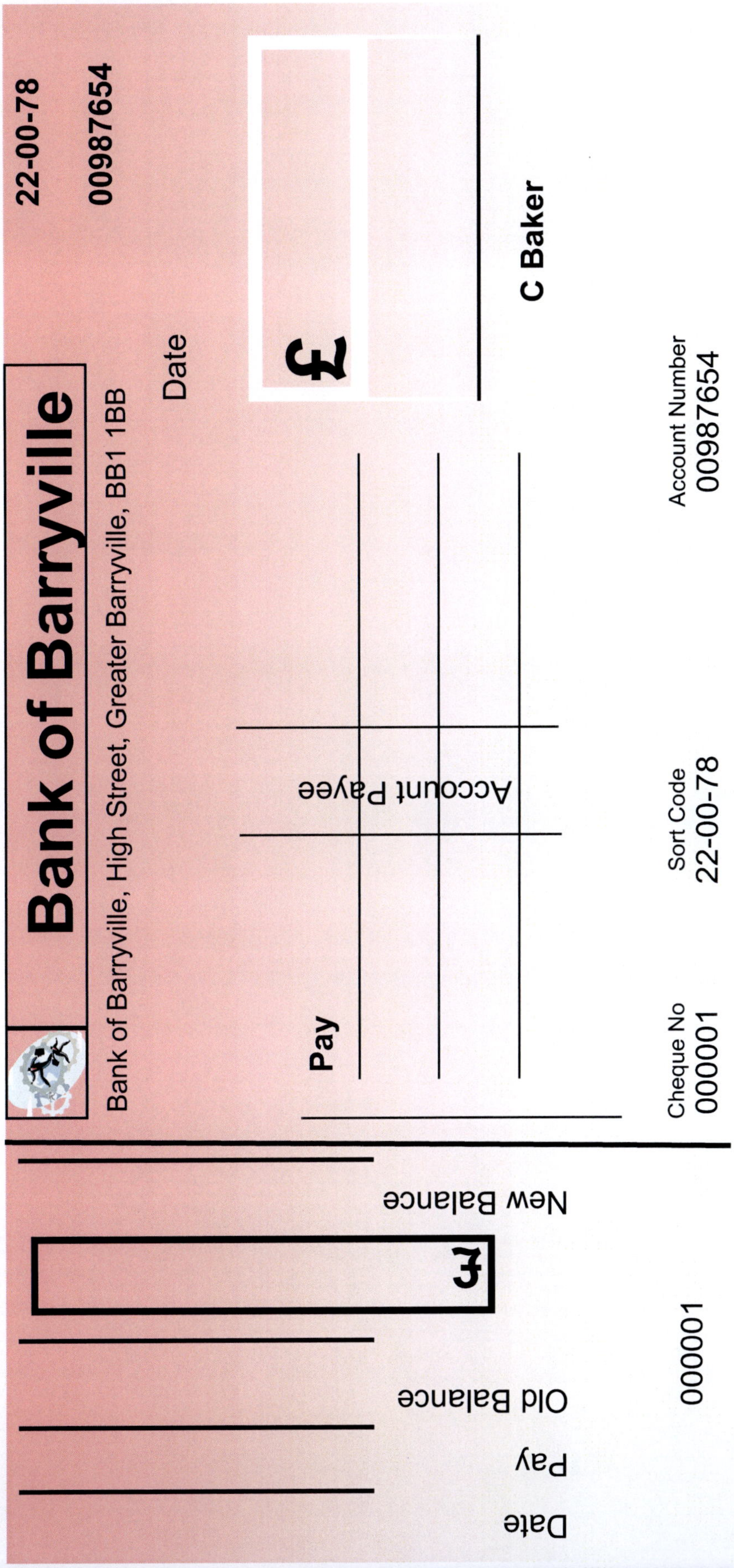

Copy ✓

# Sample paying in slip - filled in

Date *13th Jan 06*

Total Cash *£150.00*

Cheques *£200.00*

Total *£350.00*

**bank giro credit**

Date *13th Jan 06*

Cashiers

Bank: Bank of Barryville plc

Branch: Greater Barryville high Street

Account In the Name of: **C Baker**

Paid In by: *Claire Baker*

Stamp

| | | |
|---|---|---|
| £50 | *100* | *00* |
| £20 | *50* | *00* |
| £10 | | |
| £ 5 | | |
| £ 1 | | |
| 50p | | |
| 20p | | |
| Silver | | |
| Bronze | | |
| | *200* | *00* |
| | *£350.00* | |

| Sort Code | Account Number | Trans Code |
|---|---|---|
| 22-00-78 | **00987654** | **54** |

Please do not write or mark below this line

**<00987654<** **220076+** **07656544** **X**

Sample

# Sample paying in slip

Date ____________

Total Cash £ ____________

Cheques £ ____________

Total £ ____________

Date *13th Jan 06*

**bank giro credit**

Cashiers Stamp

| | |
|---|---|
| Bank | Bank of Barryville plc |
| Branch | Greater Barryville high Street |
| Account In the Name of | **C Baker** |
| Paid In by | |

| |
|---|
| £50 |
| £20 |
| £10 |
| £ 5 |
| £ 1 |
| 50p |
| 20p |
| Silver |
| Bronze |
| Total Cash |
| Cheques etc |
| £ |

| Sort Code | Account Number | Trans Code |
|---|---|---|
| 22-00-78 | **00987654** | **54** |

Please do not write or mark below this line

**<00987654<  220076+  07656544  X**

Copy ✓

Sample loan application form - filled in

# Bank of Barryville

## Loan Application Form

**Personal**

| | |
|---|---|
| **Surname** | Baker |
| **Forename (s)** | Claire |
| **Address** | 113 Treacle Terrace<br>Battenberg<br>Swiss Cottage<br>Greater Barry |
| **Postcode** | SW9 990Z |
| **Telephone Home** | 01284846209 |
| **Telephone Work** | N/a |
| **Telephone Mobile** | 077768263018 |

**Bank Details**

| | |
|---|---|
| **Name of Bank** | Bank of Barryville |
| **Address** | Town Square<br>Greater Barryville |
| **Postcode** | BB6 89DD |
| **Account Number** | 00238923 |
| **Sort Code** | 33 - 00 - 77 |
| **How long with bank** | **Years** 7 **Months** 8 |

Copy

# Bank of Barryville

## Loan Application Form

**Employment**

**Put a tick in one**

**Are you** Employed ☐ Unemployed ☐ Self Employed ✓

**Name of Company** Claire's Cakes

**Address** Treacle Terrace
Battenberg
Swiss Cottage

**Postcode** SW9 99OZ

**How long with company** Years ☐ 0

**Loan**

**Reason for the loan** To help start my own small business

**Amount of Loan** £5000.00

**To be paid back over** 60 **Months**

**At a rate of** £200.00 **Per month**

**Print Name** Claire Baker

**Signature** C Baker

**Date** 6th March 2006

Sample loan application form - filled in

Sample loan application form

# Bank of Barryville

Copy ✓

## Loan Application Form

**Personal**

| | |
|---|---|
| Surname | |
| Forename (s) | |
| Address | |
| Postcode | |
| Telephone Home | |
| Telephone Work | |
| Telephone Mobile | |

**Bank Details**

| | |
|---|---|
| Name of Bank | |
| Address | |
| Postcode | |
| Account Number | |
| Sort Code | |

| | | | | |
|---|---|---|---|---|
| How long with bank | Years | | Months | |



 

Copy ✓

# Bank of Barryville

**Employment**

**Loan Application Form**

**Put a tick in one**

**Are you** Employed ☐ Unemployed ☐ Self Employed ☐

**Name of Company** ________

**Address** ________

**Postcode** ________

**How long with company** Years ☐ Months ☐

**Loan Details**

**Reason for the loan** ________

**Amount of Loan** ________

**To be paid back over** ☐ **Months**

**At a rate of** ☐ **Per month**

**Print Name** ________

**Signature** ________

**Date** ________

**Sample loan application form**

# Sample invoice for a product

Copy ✓

**113 Treacle Terrace**
**Battenberg**
**Swiss Cottage**
**SW9 99OZ**

**Telephone: 01284846209**
**Mobile: 07768263018**
**Www.ccaps.co.uk**

# Claire's Cakes

Invoice No: 12345

8th June 2007

| Items | Cost |
|---|---|
| 1 x plastic Bride | 1.00 |
| 1 x plastic Groom | 1.00 |
| 8 x columns | 6.00 |
| 3 x tier fruit wedding cake | 110.00 |
| **Total** | **118.00** |
| **Deposit** | **28.00** |
| **Amount to pay** | **90.00** |

**Thank you for your custom**
**Claire' Cakes**



 

# Sample invoice for a service

Copy ✓

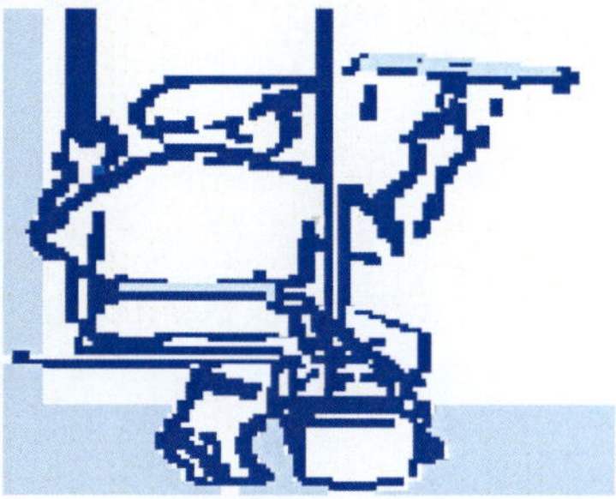

Ever Shine Window Cleaners
100 Rinse Road,
Sudingham,
B08 8LE

Tel

**Invoice Number: 123400**

**30th June 2007**

**Cleaning of windows on Humphrey House and Hector House**

**Total Amount Due £260.00 pounds**

**Payment terms as contract dated 31/12/2006**

Copy ✓

**Use this filled in invoice to help you do one for your business.**

Next page GO

| **Customer Name and Address** | **Super Screw Supplies** |
|---|---|
| **Scriven's Electrical Supplies**<br>**Electric Avenue**<br>**Shock in Watts**<br>**Shockingham**<br>**SH33 0HM** | Unit 15<br>Greater Barry Industrial Park<br>Greater Barry By–Pass<br>Greater Barry<br>United Kingdom<br>BB47 8GB<br><br>Telephone 0121444 5678<br>Fax 01214445679<br>Email<br>enquiries@supscrew.co.uk |
| **Invoice Number:**<br>**098765321** | |

| **Item Number** | Description | Quantity | Unit Price | Amount |
|---|---|---|---|---|
| 111/09867 | 6 inch flat head screw | 700 | 0.20 | 140.00 |
| 114/80765 | 6 inch Phillips screw | 700 | 0.25 | 175.00 |
| 119/08564 | 2 inch self tapping screw | 500 | 0.30 | 150.00 |
| 118/12345 | 3 inch self tapping screw | 800 | 0.35 | 280.00 |
| 110/87430 | 5 inch carriage bolts | 25 | 0.75 | 18.75 |
| 113/09099 | 1 inch counter sunk screws | 1000 | 0.10 | 100.00 |
| | | | **Total** | 863.75 |
| | | | **10% Discount** | 86.37 |
| **Thank you for shopping at SuperScrew Supplies.**<br><br>**Please call again.** | | | **Sub Total** | 777.38 |
| | | | **17.5% VAT** | 136.04 |
| | | | **Grand Total** | 913.42 |

# Blank sample invoice to fill in

Copy

| Customer Name and Address | |
|---|---|
| | |
| Invoice Number: | |

Copy

# Sample Receipts

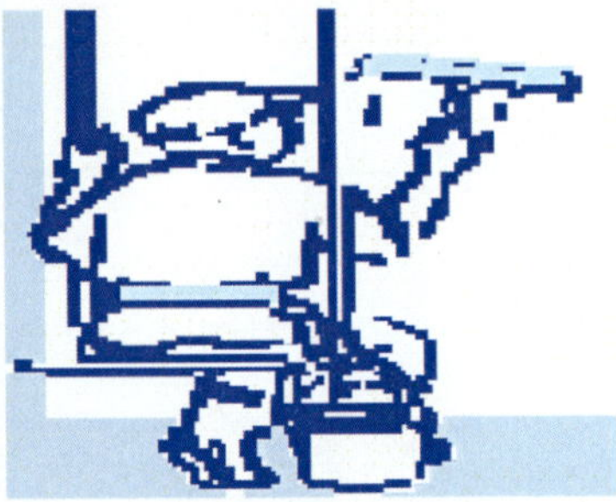

Ever Shine Window Cleaners
100 Rinse Road,
Sudingham,
B08 8LE

**Receipt Number:123401**

**16th April 2007**

**Payment received for the cleaning of 54 Rinse Road, Greater Barryville**

**£5.50**

**Thank you for using Ever Shine Window Cleaners**

113 Treacle Terrace
Battenberg
Swiss Cottage
SW9 99OZ

Telephone: 01284846209
Mobile: 07768263018
www.ccakes.co.uk

**Claire's Cakes**

**Receipt**

2nd May 2007

Payment received for the sum of

£18.00 (eighteen pounds)

Thank you Claire's Cakes

# Choose which business card is the best

**Circle the cross (X) or tick (✓)**

## Useful Tips

Copy ✓

- Keep it simple
- Make sure name, address, tel no, email etc are clear
- Is it clear what the business is?
- Use clear fonts like Arial

Look at the 5 sample cards.
Which one is the best?

The Ever Shine Windows Receipt is a clue!

X ✓

X ✓

GO

# Choose which business card is the best

Copy ✓

Circle the cross (X) or tick (✓)

Ever shine Window Cleaning Services

100 - 110 Rinse Road
Sudingham
B08 8LE

Telephone
07976273849
07972346372

X ✓

Ever shine Window Cleaning Services

100 - 110 Rinse Road
Sudingham
B08 8LE

Telephone
07976273849
07972346372

X ✓

You can use the same idea for flyers and posters

Ever shine Window Cleaning Services

**100 - 110 Rinse Road**
**Sudingham**
**B08 8LE**

**Telephone**
**07976273849**
**07972346372**

X ✓

**Birdie's Tip**

**www.vistaprint.co.uk**

# Links to more help and support

**If you live in the Black Country do get in touch with Breathing Space Ltd for help and support in setting up your business:**

**Tel: 01922 647696**
**Email; enquiries@breathingspaceltd.co.uk**
**Website: www.breathingspaceltd.co.uk**

**Other useful links to look at are:**

| | |
|---|---|
| www.businessballs.com | Help with doing a business plan and more |
| www.businesslink.gov.uk | Starting up; about all sorts of things to do with business start up |
| www.bccbl.com | Enterprise Network gives support and advice |
| www.princes-trust.org.uk | Offers Start Up in Business for young adults up to age 30. Low interest loans, test marketing grants ; free legal helpline |
| www.newbusiness.co.uk | Good site to help grow your business |
| www.smallbusinesses.co.uk | Lots of links to websites (banks, start up funding, market research) |
| www.startupcommunity.co.uk | Has help desk for people thinking of starting a business |

# Links to more help and support

**To find out more about**
**Tax, VAT, National Insurance**
**Finance for your business**
**Sales and Marketing**
**Legal Matters**
**Health and Safety**
**Business Insurance**

go to www.businesslink.gov.uk

**To find out more about help from Banks to start your Business**

| | |
|---|---|
| Barclays | www.barclays.co.uk/business |
| Natwest | www.natwest.com/newbusiness |
| Lloyds TSB | www.lloydstsbbusiness |
| HSBC | www.hsbc.co.uk/business |
| Bank of Scotland | www.bankofscotland.co.uk/business |
| Alliance and Leicester | www.alliance-leicestercommercialbank.co.uk |
| Royal Bank of Scotland | www.rbs.co.uk/smallbusiness |

**To register your business with Companies House**

www.companieshouse.gov.uk/about information and forms

**To register your business for Tax and National Insurance**

www.hmrc.gov.uk/startingup/register

# Books and Software

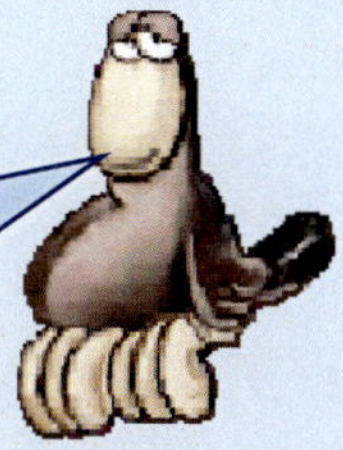

If this book has been of help to you why not have a look at the workbook, DVD and CD Rom.

## Other material produced by Breathing Space Ltd on Enterprise Support

- Reading, Writing and Maths for Self Employment Workbook
- Reading, Writing and Maths for Self Employment CD Rom
- 7C's Women Into Business Toolkit (Book and DVD)

# The End!

**We hope you have found this toolkit helpful.**

**We hope it has given you a good idea of how to do a Business Plan.**

**This toolkit does not deal with all the ins and outs of business planning.**

**If you do want to go on to set up your own business it is best to ask for advice from a professional business advisor.**

*Birdie*

Business Birdie has flown the nest!
Be sure to make your business the best!